"*I Was a Stranger* reveals Jodi Fondell's pastoral heart and her stirring passion for justice. Drawing on her vast personal experience in international churches, Jodi is able to say what needs to be said about the call to Christian people to welcome the stranger. As Jodi sees it, this call isn't just a nice, but largely peripheral, dimension to ministry; this call is at the heart of the gospel."

—**Douglas Brouwer**
author of *How to Become a Multicultural Church*

"A gifted colleague in cross-cultural ministry, Jodi Fondell puts into words what many of us international pastors passionately want to share with the larger church: God is glorified whenever you welcome the stranger! And here's the real surprise: you are blessed whenever you welcome the stranger! Here is a helpful guide for congregations who desire to become a more faithful and hospitable sanctuary for all God's people."

—**Scott Herr**
Senior Pastor, American Church in Paris

"Isolation beyond your control is a very cruel space to exist within. In this exquisitely-written, timely, and poignant wake-up call for Christians, Jodi challenges us to reexamine our prejudices when it comes to alienating others—both consciously and subconsciously. Through resonant personal anecdotes that provide perspective and comparison, as well as practical tips for chipping away at bias and tools for integration, she implores us to develop our compassion and empathy as we live out our faith in these trying times."

—**Lola Akinmade Åkerström**
award-winning author and photographer of bestselling
LAGOM: The Swedish Secret of Living Well

"Jodi Mullen Fondell provides an accessible and timely look at understanding and practicing the vital biblical mandate to welcome strangers, foreigners, and all those persons whom others may shun or even hate. From her years of pastoral ministry within international communities, Mullen Fondell invites us to embrace this central individual and communal Christian calling, which demonstrates the overflowing love of God in Christ that to all who find themselves as the outsider and outcast."

—**Edwin David Aponte**
Executive Director, Louisville Institute

"Jodie Fondell's *I Was a Stranger* touches anyone who has ever felt on the outside, yearns to connect in a congregational setting and seeks to make sense of their identity in the world today. She shares personal narratives, integrates theology and Scripture, and applies it to daily life within various congregational contexts. Wherever we serve, Jodie encourages faith communities to live out our vocational call as we find new ways to welcome, include, and love our neighbor."

—**Pastor Emily G. Rova-Hegener**
American Lutheran Congregation, Oslo, Norway

I WAS A STRANGER

I Was a Stranger

Encouraging the Church to Welcome and Embrace the Foreigner

Jodi Mullen Fondell

Foreword by Mark A. Labberton

RESOURCE *Publications* • Eugene, Oregon

I WAS A STRANGER
Encouraging the Church to Welcome and Embrace the Foreigner

Copyright © 2019 Jodi Mullen Fondell. All rights reserved. Except for brief quotations in critical publications or reviews, no part of this book may be reproduced in any manner without prior written permission from the publisher. Write: Permissions, Wipf and Stock Publishers, 199 W. 8th Ave., Suite 3, Eugene, OR 97401.

Resource Publications
An Imprint of Wipf and Stock Publishers
199 W. 8th Ave., Suite 3
Eugene, OR 97401

www.wipfandstock.com

PAPERBACK ISBN: 978-1-5326-7958-2
HARDCOVER ISBN: 978-1-5326-7959-9
EBOOK ISBN: 978-1-5326-7960-5

Manufactured in the U.S.A.   JULY 26, 2019

Scripture quotations are taken from the Holy Bible, New Living Translation, copyright ©1996, 2004, 2015 by Tyndale House Foundation. Used by permission of Tyndale House Publishers, Inc., Carol Stream, Illinois 60188. All rights reserved

"Aliens, Strangers and Gospel," Chawkat Georges Moucarry, used with the permission of www.intervarsity.org.

"The Problem with the Melting Pot," Miguel De La Torre, used with the permission of www.ethicsdaily.com

This work is dedicated to my husband Douglas, my partner in life, my co-worker in ministry, my soulmate in all things. Thanks for sharing the journey with me.

Contents

Foreword by Mark A. Labberton | ix
Acknowledgements | xi
Introduction | xv

1. Recognize God's Concern for the Foreigner | 1
2. Identify with the Stranger | 8
3. Understand with Compassion | 20
4. Realize Who Moves | 31
5. Grasp the Great Opportunity | 45
6. Count the Costs | 49
7. Welcome Visitors In | 54
8. Distinguish Between Integration and Assimilation | 67
9. Practice Meaningful Integration | 81
10. Celebrate Together! | 96
11. Embrace the Wider World of Christianity | 102
12. Share the Good News | 112

Small Group Guide | 117
For Further Study | 131
Bibliography | 133

Foreword

WHAT YOU HOLD IN your hands is a rich and inspiring gift. It is the witness of someone who leads by example in doing what all, especially followers of Jesus, are invited to do: to see and hear and welcome the stranger.

In a time of global fear about the intense and diverse world we share, Jodi Mullen Fondell speaks expansively and passionately about what it means "to love our neighbors as ourselves." Here she shares her wonderful journey of learning and growing in her capacity to step towards and not away from the neighbor who may seem strange or foreign. She and her husband Doug have chosen to open doors and to cross thresholds, in turn welcoming immigrants and refugees to do likewise.

What is so helpful about Jodi's inspirational account is how she shows us that such hospitality needn't require extra degrees, but rather something more profound and already within our capacity: a genuinely open, empathetic heart and mind. We do not need to concentrate on changing who we are so much as we can purpose to be taken up in the joyful and complex discovery of who our immigrant, displaced neighbors are. Therein lies the gift of God to us and through us.

Fondell makes it clear, of course, that such neighbor-love may not always be natural or easy. There is a price. But in sum, the price is overwhelmingly outmeasured by the greater gain of being in relationship with our neighbor and of sharing in the heart of God who loves us both. Herein lies the core of the truth and grace Jodi

Mullen Fondell explores so practically and personally: we are all aliens, strangers, foreigners, immigrants and, astoundingly, God in Christ pursues, welcomes, includes, and loves us all. How then can we who have received such capacious love do anything but try and mirror it back to God and to all those made invaluably in God's image?

This is the embodied witness of love, mercy, and justice that is meant to be the evidence in our alienated world that the God of reconciliation in Christ has a family of reconciled people whose lives and love continuously invite others to "taste and see that the Lord is good."

Thank you, Jodi Mullen Fondell, for this amazing and fresh invitation! Reading it, may we respond by entering into and sharing the feast of God's great love.

—MARK A. LABBERTON
President, Fuller Theological Seminary

Acknowledgements

WRITING HAS ALWAYS FIGURED prominently in my life, whether it was through the short stories I wrote as a child; the copious journals that I kept throughout high school, college, and beyond; the sermons that I have written for my work as a pastor; or the blog that I started in 2008 to satisfy a yearning to share my thoughts about all manner of things. Writing has helped me find my voice and hone my perspectives on things trivial as well as on ideas that truly matter. I always hoped I would find my way to getting a book written and now that that hope has become a reality, I am truly grateful beyond measure.

We do not reach for our dreams and accomplish our goals in isolation, but rather in the company of all who love and encourage us. The joy of publishing this book is slightly diminished by my sorrow that my parents are not here on this earth to celebrate the accomplishment with me. Ted and Rose Ann Mullen offered a very wide embrace to all people, regardless of their background or situation in life. They were the ultimate lovers of people and their legacy remains with all who knew them and enjoyed being loved by them. As the chief beneficiary of this unconditional love, I remain forever grateful for the encouragement they always gave me to be whoever I wanted to be. They also modeled how to have ambition, but never at the cost of other humans. I bear full responsibility for whatever failure I have exhibited in this regard.

I am deeply appreciative of the Louisville Institute in Louisville, Kentucky, who granted me a Pastoral Study Grant in 2017

ACKNOWLEDGEMENTS

that provided the funding I needed to set aside time from other work to pursue the vision for this book. The collaborative weekend with other grantees along with the ongoing support I have received from the Institute is deeply appreciated.

I am grateful for the American International Church in London, England; the English Speaking United Methodist church in Vienna, Austria; the All Nations Church Luxembourg; and the American Church in Paris, France for the warm interactions during my visits to conduct interviews, and for their stories which informed this work. Their respective pastors, Jennifer Mills-Knutsen, Matthew Lafferty, Paul McMinnimy and Scott Herr were invaluable in pulling people together to share their experiences with me.

Special thanks goes out to Mark Labberton, whom I first met in Paris at a conference for pastors serving international churches. Mark's insights about building community and loving our neighbors have inspired my own thinking in deep and influential ways. I am grateful he took time out of his demanding schedule to write the foreword for this book.

I would also like to thank Douglas Brouwer, a colleague in international ministry and trusted friend who gave me inestimable counsel on the publishing process and the encouragement necessary to complete it.

Through their comments over the years, the regular readers of my blog have heartened me to keep with the craft and pushed me to write even more.

My thanks to them and all my readers and cheerleaders, including Zena Martin, a member of the London church, whose interest in my first tentative pages inspired me to press forward. Marie Grout, a member of our Stockholm church and the church in Paris, thought she'd mosey through the chapters I'd sent her, but ended up devouring the whole thing in one sitting. Tom and Deb Cowger recognized the beauty in the narratives of people who have been embraced by a loving church community and convinced me that these stories needed to be told. I'd like to say a deeply heartfelt thank you to the Rev. Dr. Scott Herr, with whom I was privileged

ACKNOWLEDGEMENTS

to work at the American Church in Paris from March 2017-January 2018. Scott pushed me to write and then provided valuable feedback when I finally presented him with something coherent! Many thanks to Jenn Cavanaugh, whom I first met through her daughter's participation in our youth group at the American Church in Paris, for her insightful editorial work in preparing this text for publication. A quintet of women from my Stockholm days read pieces of the manuscript when I needed other eyes on my words. Marilyn Bojler, Sandra Carpenter, Bert Curtis, Mary Jane Segerlund, and Judy Vlastnik: I'm not sure how to express my deep gratitude for all that you did to help me reach the finish line. *Stora kramar till er alla*! I am indebted to Matthew Wimer at Wipf and Stock for guiding me through this first book and granting me the opportunity to publish with them. Any errors that remain in this book are solely my own.

The most significant group of people who birthed this work in me are the dear people of Immanuel International in Stockholm, Sweden. For all who attended our church from September 1998-December of 2014, this volume is really written as a love letter to you. You have shaped my life in ways that I continue to find compelling by living out in concrete actions the deep hospitality that God longs for us to show every human we encounter. You trekked with me as we followed God's lead on this road of empowering the church to be a place of warm embrace and a shining beacon of light and hope in an often cold and desolate Nordic country. The words written in every bulletin during our time there remain with me as a mantra for what I long the church to be world-wide: a place where no matter your situation, you are welcome, for God is our gracious host. To all who participated in the significant round table conversations that I held during 2017, I am indebted. It is your stories that illustrate the beauty of an open church. Every word that is contained in this book is written with you in my heart, and I remain humbled by the privilege it was for me to be one of your pastors for almost seventeen years. While once strangers, we are now family, knit together with the lasting and deep love of Jesus.

ACKNOWLEDGEMENTS

And last, but certainly not least, is Douglas, my co-laborer in the gospel, my husband, my soulmate, my one and only. Life in ministry would never have been as fruitful and as fun as it has been with you by my side. From your initial encouragement to apply for the grant, and then sharing my joy in getting it, to the support you have shown me as I endeavored to write this book, and then believing that I could actually finish it, helped me to cross the finish line. Thank you for walking alongside of me, for celebrating me, for loving me so deeply and without condition. Your wide embrace of me and your deep love for humanity inspires me to continue to want to be a better person. It is with deep gratitude that in the year we celebrate 25 years of marriage, I dedicate this work to you, the one who has practiced the principles and embodied the ideals outlined here all of the years we've shared in ministry together.

To God be the glory. And may the church glorify the God who welcomes the stranger, loves the immigrant, shows favor to the marginalized, and embraces all comers by following in those deep and wide footsteps.

Pentecost 2019

Introduction

I HAVE PACKED UP my life and moved to a foreign country on five different occasions; six, if you count rural Alaska as a foreign country—which in 1981, as a girl from Southern California, I certainly did. In fact, I am putting the finishing touches on this manuscript while on a temporary assignment in Luxembourg. As has been the case with most of my moves, I knew only a handful of people living in this foreign land that I was to make home. And yet, I was buoyed by the knowledge that an international church would once again be at the center of my life and work.

I am a social creature by nature, the very definition of an extrovert. I crave connection. Living without a community that knows me well feels like a death sentence for me. As a person of faith, whenever feelings of isolation overwhelm me, I naturally look to the church to find community, acceptance, and encouragement. One would think that the church would be rock solid in these areas, but truth be told, the church can fall woefully short of its calling to welcome the stranger. The old saying about birds of a feather flocking together often holds as true in the church as in the wild. It's kind of ironic. Many show up at church looking for connection and community, but sadly, once it's found, the instinct can be to close off the opening for others to find the same. Most people love finding community but have a harder time leaving the community open to newcomers. We like the safety of our established communities, especially ones that look like we do, act like we do, and fall in line with how we think.

INTRODUCTION

The problem with the church operating from this perspective is that it is not at all what Christ ever intended for his church. Christ intends that the doors of his church always be wide open to all, and mostly particularly to those coming from outside of our expected and established ways of looking, acting, and thinking—those whom the Bible refers to as strangers. In my opinion, as well as in my experience, the gospel is clearly demonstrated in acts of hospitality.

I know at the most visceral level what it means to be a stranger and a foreigner. It leaves one feeling vulnerable and lonely. I also know firsthand that the church can play an important role in countering these feelings of alienation. Prior to my first call way back in 1998, I had only a limited understanding of the role of hospitality in church ministry. I had lived in Colombia before attending seminary, and although I was not part of an international church while there, I was privileged to experience local Colombian churches as a congregant, which expanded my view of the worldwide church. The next four occasions that I moved to a foreign land and found myself in the stranger seat once again, I did so as a pastor, called to lead various international congregations in Europe. My first call was to co-pastor, alongside my husband Doug, the International Fellowship of Immanuel Church in Stockholm, Sweden. Immanuel Church is a unique congregation situated in the heart of Stockholm. Motivated by a desire to provide places of worship and fellowship for immigrant groups for whom worshipping in Swedish was difficult, this Swedish church started outreach ministries to the Korean community and the English-speaking populations in Stockholm. The vision was for Immanuel to be one church with three language groups.

Thrilled with the possibility of leading an international congregation, we eagerly prepared for our move to Sweden. In our minds, we'd sign a three-year contract, maybe spend five years at the most living in Europe, then come back to our "real life" in the US. Well, that initial three-year contract turned into almost seventeen years with this amazing congregation that opened up my heart, my mind, and my eyes to a world of Christian ministry that

INTRODUCTION

had been previously hidden from me in my monocultural world. From my pastoral vantage point I saw how a congregation that embraced its calling to be a place of hospitality and community, especially for the foreigner, reflected more fully all that God desired for the church. Welcoming the stranger and embracing the foreigner became the lifeblood of this church's ministry and instilled in me a deep desire to tell the stories of what God is doing through this and other international churches in Europe, in the hopes that they will inspire other churches in their ministry to the outsider.

I can honestly say that what sat at the heart of our ministry was hospitality, being a welcoming community, a place where foreigners could be seen and heard and be called stranger no more. These international congregations in Europe have transformed my life and shaped and touched the lives of countless others. My view of how deeply God loves the whole wide world expanded through experiencing the joy of seeing expatriates and refugees worshipping and praying together within the walls of these churches. International churches invite wealthy top dogs of multi-national companies to break bread with newspaper delivery men and taxicab drivers. At the foot of Christ's cross, we find level ground. As lonely sojourners in need of community and wayward sinners in need of a savior, each of us found the deepest level of community and unity with people who looked different from us, grew up in different socio-economic situations than we did, and came from religious traditions different from our own. The great surprise was that it was not a recipe for conflict but instead a place where profound and unexpected connections took place. The ultimate gift was living into our dream of becoming a place that reflected heaven itself.

Honest reflection on my experience in international ministry entails not only rejoicing in the good, but also looking back critically on areas in which I have seen the church fall short of its calling. Because so much of my experience transpired there, most of not only the success stories, but also the cautionary tales are drawn from our time at Immanuel, the church I helped to pastor in Stockholm, Sweden. I write only from my perspective, and

xvii

INTRODUCTION

therefore from a flawed and limited point of view. Others would comment on the same situations in entirely different ways. However, even as I seek to learn from some of the painful times, what lingers is a deep and lasting joy for the opportunity to have been a part of this church for almost seventeen years, and I remain utterly grateful for this place and its people.

My passion for this topic is borne out of seeing God's word in action through the beautiful and faithful people I have been privileged to serve alongside of in the various churches I have pastored. Rather than approaching the subject from a scholarly standpoint, I hope to offer glimpses of how the often uncomfortable work of embracing the other is worth it, and to witness to the truth that God's word does not return void. While I cite places in scripture where I see a message of embrace, a calling to love the outsider, this book focuses on the experiences which lead me to believe that God wants us to welcome those who find themselves lacking a place of belonging in this world. I offer the testimony of people and churches who have embodied the biblical call to welcome in concrete and meaningful ways, with encouragement along the way for all of us to grow our own generosity of spirit toward the stranger and foreigner in our midst. I have included a study guide that invites readers to a deeper study of certain biblical passages that I think are germane to this conversation.

This book invites individuals and churches alike to join the journey that begins with encountering strangers, shifts to calling them friends, and endures by embracing one another as brother and sister because of the deep bond formed through the love of God in Christ. As you listen to the stories of the people of God, and consider the practical tips offered, I pray that your empathy for those finding themselves as strangers in a strange land will increase and that you will discover the deep joy of doing the hard work necessary to open wide the doors of your community.

1

Recognize God's Concern for the Foreigner

IN MATTHEW 25:34-36, JESUS tells the parable of the sheep and the goats. In this image of sorting the righteous from the unrighteous, we see Christ's criteria for a virtuous lifestyle.

> Then the King will say to those on his right, "Come, you who are blessed by my Father, inherit the Kingdom prepared for you from the creation of the world. For I was hungry, and you fed me. I was thirsty, and you gave me a drink. I was a stranger, and you invited me into your home. I was naked, and you gave me clothing. I was sick, and you cared for me. I was in prison, and you visited me."

The people listening are a bit confused and they ask when they ever did these things for Jesus. Jesus answers that whenever they fed the hungry, gave drink to the thirsty, welcomed the stranger, clothed the sick, and cared for the poor of our world, they were doing it for Jesus. The great surprise of this parable is that so many people who thought they were righteous discover that in Christ's eyes they are not because they have failed to show compassion for those most vulnerable in our world. At the most basic level, this parable reveals to us that as Christians, the way we care for the poor and welcome the stranger are direct reflections of how well we doing at serving Jesus.

Welcoming the stranger is a key theme throughout the Bible. Many sections of the biblical narrative reveal to us that God has a soft and tender heart towards those who identify as strangers. This isn't that surprising since large portions of the Old Testament revolve around people who find themselves exiled in one way or another. Today, people have various motives for going into exile, or on the move, landing in a new and different place. Most often, they stem from a desire to find a better life than their native homeland offers. Reasons for this include wars, poor infrastructure, broken school systems, high unemployment, dishonest politicians, oppressive caste systems, and persecution for holding differing religious and political beliefs than those in power. Life is often hard for people who seek out a better life in a new nation.

God's word directs our attention to how to care for those finding themselves in exile. The Old Testament includes thirty-six commands to love the alien and the stranger. Here is a small sampling of some of the biblical texts that have compelled me to consider how this theme should impact our church ministries:

- "Do not take advantage of foreigners who live among you in your land. Treat them like native-born Israelites, and love them as you love yourself. Remember that you were once foreigners living in the land of Egypt. I am the Lord your God" (Leviticus 19:33-34).

- "Do not oppress widows, orphans, foreigners, and the poor. And do not scheme against each other" (Zechariah 7:10).

- "At that time I will put you on trial. I am eager to witness against all sorcerers and adulterers and liars. I will speak against those who cheat employees of their wages, who oppress widows and orphans, or who deprive the foreigners living among you of justice, for these people do not fear me, says the Lord of Heaven's Armies" (Malachi 3:5).

RECOGNIZE GOD'S CONCERN FOR THE FOREIGNER

- "The Lord protects the foreigners among us. He cares for the orphans and widows, but he frustrates the plans of the wicked" (Psalm 146:9).
- "You must not mistreat or oppress foreigners in any way. Remember, you yourselves were once foreigners in the land of Egypt" (Exodus 22:21).
- "You must not oppress foreigners. You know what it's like to be a foreigner, for you yourselves were once foreigners in the land of Egypt" (Exodus 23:9).

The story of Ruth is a deeply touching narrative that many Christians treasure, but have you considered that it is, at its core, a story of refugees seeking the kindness of those to whom they were mere strangers?

Based on all this, I am led to believe that God's command to us is to be kind to foreigners, or at the very least, to not exploit them. As followers of God, we are called to offer rest, relief, and restoration to those who are in exile, including foreigners lacking a sense of belonging and outsiders who are vulnerable and lack a sense of rootedness. We are certainly not to exacerbate their condition by treating them with hostility, ignoring their needs, or by asking them to return to their homelands, no matter what drove them out. I believe that God's word exhibits a great love for the foreigner, and therefore deem it fitting that the church care for those in that position. We need to remember that life is hard for people who are displaced, often for reasons outside of their control. George Moucarry sums it up well.

> The Mosaic law frequently associates aliens and strangers with widows, orphans, the poor, and the Levites. This emphasizes that a foreigner's life is not an easy one. His work is often hard and poorly paid, and he may not be able to afford good housing. In addition to any material difficulties he may face, there are emotional challenges: he is an uprooted person, deprived of the comfort of his native language, family and friends. In short, he is alone. This loneliness is all the more painful because it is seldom a personal choice, hence the tendency for

foreigners to stick together. They attempt thereby to recreate a bit of their home environment. The more different the home country is from the new country, the more leaving home seems like going into exile. Sometimes this exile can motivate foreigners to try to integrate into their new society. But more often it has the opposite effect and makes them vulnerable, in some cases even to the point of becoming victims or perpetrators of criminal activity. Because exile causes suffering, God has a special love for aliens and strangers. In his well-known prophetic description of the last judgement in Matthew 25:35, Jesus, by associating the foreigner with the hungry, thirsty, the naked, the sick, and the prisoners, draws our attention to the precarious living conditions of the foreigners. Jesus is not preaching salvation by works in this text, but he clearly shows us that true belief in him necessarily manifests itself in acts of solidarity toward those most in need, including foreigners.[1]

Scripture references how to care for the foreigner, not only because the Israelites had experienced exile, but also in part due to the reality that the Israelites were dealing with foreigners in their midst as well. Almost as soon as they settled in the Promised Land, the people of Israel found themselves faced with the question of what to do about foreigners. Among the foreigners living in Israel were those who had accompanied them on their flight from Egypt. At the time of King Solomon there were about 150,000 such aliens in Israel, about a tenth of the country's total population. As is usual today, most of these were unskilled workers. They were exploited for cheap and hard labor and this led to a difficult life laced with suffering.[2] The church has not fully allowed these narratives to shape it in its role in ministering to those who find themselves as strangers in a strange land. People moving from their homelands to a new land is not a new concept, and yet in many ways

---

1. Moucarry, "Aliens, Strangers, and the Gospel", https://ism.intervarsity.org/resource/aliens-strangers-and-gospel
2. 2 Chronicles 2:17, 8:7–8

Christians have failed to see how difficult life is for foreigners and subsequently have ignored the call to care for them.

I find it interesting that Scripture also encourages those who move to a new homeland to invest in that place and to work hard at making the strange place a home. It's hard and it's costly, but it is indeed the best way. Consider Abram/Abraham and Sarah. In Genesis 12:1 we hear God say to Abram, "Leave your native country and your relatives, and go to the land that I will show you." Later, in verse ten, we see the following turn of events: "At that time a severe famine struck the land of Canaan, forcing Abram to go down to Egypt, where he lived as a foreigner." There's also Joseph, who was sold to people from another country through no fault of his own but went on to accomplish amazing things.[3] Consider Jeremiah the prophet telling a captive, exiled people to invest in the land of their captivity.

> This is what the Lord of Heaven's Armies, the God of Israel, says to all the captives he has exiled to Babylon from Jerusalem: "Build homes, and plan to stay. Plant gardens, and eat the food they produce. Marry and have children. Then find spouses for them so that you may have many grandchildren. Multiply! Do not dwindle away! And work for the peace and prosperity of the city where I sent you into exile. Pray to the Lord for it, for its welfare will determine your welfare" (Jeremiah 29:5–7).

We can see that people moving from one homeland to another is a phenomenon that has been unfolding throughout history. I note a call for those on the move to settle in and embrace their new dwelling as home. I also see a great opportunity, especially for the church, when encountering foreigners in their homeland, to care for and embrace the new people in their midst.

These biblical narratives still resonate today. People moving from their homelands do so most often to seek a better life for their families. Controversy abounds around the topic of immigration. As Christians, I believe that we have a great opportunity to care for the foreigner in our midst as a clear display of God's love.

3. See Genesis 37 and following.

Being exiled and finding yourself living as a stranger in a strange land inevitably brings loneliness and vulnerability. People in these circumstances often face life without extended family or land ownership, which was just as essential to a comfortable lifestyle in the Old Testament economy as it is today. Exploiting the deep needs that emerge among people living on the fringes of society was just as easy then as it is today. That is, in part, why the thirty-six commands set forth in the Old Testament were given: to provide some level of protection from the vulnerabilities that these people faced day in, day out. God saw this and commanded the people of God to behave in a generous and loving manner, not with harsh actions that pushed the foreigner down. Do we not also have a responsibility to offer care and compassion to today's foreigner?

A beautiful image of the perfect harmony that God intends for humanity is found in Revelation.

> After this I saw a vast crowd, too great to count, from every nation and tribe and people and language, standing in front of the throne and before the Lamb. They were clothed in white robes and held palm branches in their hands. And they were shouting with a great roar, "Salvation comes from our God who sits on the throne and from the Lamb!" And all the angels were standing around the throne and around the elders and the four living beings. And they fell before the throne with their faces to the ground and worshiped God. They sang, "Amen! Blessing and glory and wisdom and thanksgiving and honor and power and strength belong to our God forever and ever! Amen"(Revelation.7:9–12).

When I read these verses, I am moved to ask, as Christians, what is our responsibility to work toward that image of all nations, tribes, and peoples finding unity by welcoming people from all nations to our churches?

God's demonstrated compassion and care for the foreigner and the stranger has led me to believe that we should cultivate a desire to welcome and embrace people in those circumstances as well. Little doubt exists about the reality that we are mired in a confusing conversation right now, especially in the United States where disagreements over immigration policy and border control are dominating the political landscape. But the US isn't the only place where these disputes are unfolding. Many European countries also feel a tug back to a protectionist mentality where a growing number of people favor a more closed society. The politics of immigration are complex; but rather than getting bogged down in the debates around legal and illegal immigration, let's focus on the church's role in caring for those whose very lives are impacted by policies that leave them in a very difficult and often painful place, between two worlds, neither of which offers them a hopeful future.

As Christ-followers, we are called to cultivate a knowledge of what it means to answer God's call to care for and welcome the foreigner and the stranger. At the very least, we should nurture a deep and abiding concern for the welfare of these people, viewing them as children of God and not just pawns in a political battle. Moving toward a place of deeper understanding for why people would move to a foreign country, often without permission, while risking everything to do so is the first step in being able to welcome and embrace the strangers in our midst. One of the ways that we can do this is through building empathy with those who are displaced from their homeland by remembering when we too were strangers. God urged the Hebrews to show compassion to the foreigners in their midst in part because they knew firsthand what it was like to be a foreigner, since they had once been foreigners in the land of Egypt. God exhorts them to recall the days when they were the outsiders and to allow the memories of being the oppressed people to spur them on to greater compassion when encountering others in a similar situation. Recalling our own moments of alienation assist us in the same task.

2

Identify with the Stranger

Remember Your Alienation

WHILE GOD URGES THE Israelites to remember that they were also once foreigners in order to stir their empathy for the foreigner in their midst, it's not the only reason that God calls his people to remember. Remembering, or not forgetting, is an important theme in the Old Testament. The command to remember is central to the theology of the book of Deuteronomy, especially as it pertains to the sojourner. The warning not to forget the past underscores that imperative.[1] The concept of raising an *ebenezer* is also prominent in the Old Testament narrative. Perhaps you have sung about raising your *ebenezer* and wondered what it is you were actually singing about. While it is a foreign concept to today's reader, it was deeply meaningful to the Israelites. Chapters 4–7 of 1 Samuel describe a series of battles between the Israelites and the Philistines. As a reminder of the great victory God gave to Israel during the battle at Eben Ezer, Samuel took a great stone and raised it as a memorial between Misspell and Shen. Samuel then took a large stone and placed it between the towns of Mizpah and Jeshanah. He named it Ebenezer (which means "the stone of

---

1. For a fuller discussion of Deuteronomy, see Carroll, *For Our Good Always*, 441–61.

help"), for he said, "Up to this point the Lord has helped us!"(1 Samuel 7:12). Whenever the Israelites looked at the stone from that point on, they would remember how God had helped them.

When we sing about raising an *ebenezer* we are poetically referencing this story along with our own memories of God's help in times of trouble.

Remembering helps us to recall the ways in which God has delivered us in times of trial and peril, giving us strength to face the challenges ahead of us. Remembering helps us to remain firm when our faith is shaken. Remembering also helps us to build empathy, and this is what God is driving at when he commands the Israelites to remember their own exile when tempted to deal with the strangers in their midst in less than kind and generous ways.

In many ways the discipline of remembering is an important aspect of helping us to grow. As we remember how we coped when we encountered a certain situation before, we are given the opportunity to repeat what ultimately proved to be helpful or to do things differently in the hopes of a better outcome. At the very least, perhaps we manage the stress better than we did originally, having grown in faith that such difficulties are survivable. Anytime we experience feelings of stress or disorientation, our memory helps us recall other times when we felt this way and got through it. Our hard-earned hindsight assures us that this too shall pass. It is God's desire for us to remember significant moments when we knew God was present and active. It gives us confidence that since God showed up then, we can have faith that God will indeed show up once more.

Take Stock on the Journey

In conjunction with remembering where we have once been is this notion of being on a continual journey of growth and change. We are embarking upon a journey together, a journey that will ask you to remember your own stories, and urge you to begin to see others' through more compassionate lenses. The hope is that you will begin to cultivate God's heart for others in your own heart instead of hanging onto safe assumptions that foster preconceived yet erroneous points of view. In order to do that we need to be willing to try new things and enter new worlds.

Truth be told, entering new worlds used to sound more enjoyable to me than it does nowadays. Experiencing a foreign place can be exhilarating, but the process of getting there is rarely fun. Gone are the halcyon days of exotic and exciting plane travel. Now it really is just a modernized cattle car, a means of getting from point A to point B. Expecting it to be enjoyable rarely enters my mind anymore. With each boarding card that I print, I find myself just hoping the experience won't be too painful—and this is for trips to self-chosen destinations rather than anything forced upon me by difficult circumstances. I remember one trip in particular, being packed like sardines into a completely full 747. I had not been looking forward to the twelve-hour flight between Frankfurt, Germany and Los Angeles, California anyway; then to make matters worse, I was seated by the window in a row with two large men blocking my way to the aisle. I felt trapped. The guy in the middle was trying to squeeze out a bit more room than his allotted space allowed so we found ourselves elbow wrestling on the armrest between seats. I had to establish a firm perimeter with my legs so that his legs wouldn't drift into my space. The final straw, however, was when he fell asleep, mouth wide open, head turned towards mine, exhaling his stinky, hot breath right onto my neck! Air travel creates such bizarre, unwanted intimacies between us and those with whom fly.

But on this very same flight, a delightful thing occurred as well. An elderly man was in the middle seat in the row in front of me. Suddenly, I saw his arms fly up into the air. He had decided to begin a series of seated stretches mid-flight! It wasn't long before his seatmates and several others joined in on this impromptu exercise class. All these synchronized arms popping up and down, in and out of my field of vision brought a smile to my face and gave me some relief from the unpleasantness of my own seating arrangement. We need to remember that most journeys are like this, sometimes filled with unexpected laughter, kindnesses, and joy, but also filled with headaches and difficulties that stress us out and cause us anxiety. The journey of learning to identify with the outsider might feel like being packed into a metal tube like a sardine with a stranger breathing down your neck. Opening ourselves up to seeing something through new and different lenses is often difficult and sometimes painful. But it also produces growth and allows us to open ourselves up to the work that God wants to do in our lives. As we develop a more welcome attitude toward the strangers in our midst, at some point we'll also catch the joy of the unexpected connections and end up feeling encouraged, even energized, by new perspectives.

A journey can be simply defined as the act of traveling from one place to another. It's also a process, likened to traveling; a passage. Whatever the definition, all things related to a journey indicate movement, going from one place to another. This can be literal, like when we travel, or metaphorical, like when we go through something significant in life. Both physical journeys and life journeys are planned and unplanned, often challenging, riddled with unexpected twists and turns but also sometimes laced with joys and kindnesses that we most likely did not expect. Many clichés exist about journeys and destinations but the reason for there being so few "destination" moments in life where we feel we have truly "arrived" is because there is always room to grow, always an opportunity to go just a little deeper. This holds especially true in our spiritual lives. What God is doing through each and every day of our lives, in any given moment even, is perhaps more important than any end result. When do we ever feel that we've truly arrived in our spiritual lives? Rejoice that you are on a journey! Being on a journey indicates movement and without movement we do not grow or change.

Identify Feelings of Disorientation

It's important to note that with movement and change, feelings of disorientation emerge. We move outside of our comfort zones and are faced with myriad issues that are foreign to us. When we travel somewhere new, literally or figuratively, these feelings of disorientation can overwhelm us. I lived in Sweden for almost seventeen years. While living there I did a decent job of learning the language, and fortunately, whenever I couldn't quite sort out the Swedish, loads of folks spoke English. Stockholm is a clean, beautiful, well-ordered, well-run city. All in all, it was a fairly easy place to dip one's toe into the world of foreign living. For all intents and purposes, I felt at home—mostly. I say mostly because, well, even identifying where home is can create a sort of ambiguity inside of me. Whenever I left Sweden to travel to the US, I spoke of going home. Then while I was in the US, I referred to my return to Sweden as going home. While this seems to be a contradiction of terms, it's really not a contradiction—it's more of a conundrum. Where is that place that I call home? Talk about disorientation.

In fact, the experience of feeling like a foreigner was equally confounding in both places. There were days when, even after living in Stockholm for almost seventeen years, I still felt like I'd just arrived. I couldn't figure out where to find something at the grocery store. Swedish sounded like gibberish to me and I couldn't follow a conversation let alone formulate the sentences necessary to participate coherently. One quirk of Swedish society is an obsession with queue numbers. In most stores, one has to obtain a queue number in order to be served. No matter if you are the first customer to enter said establishment in two days. Even after all my years of living there, I would often walk into a Swedish shop and wait patiently in line, only to be pushed aside by a Swede with their little queue number. Every time, I would roll my eyes in disgust, feeling angry with both the system and myself for not remembering how to work the system even after all those years! Two years after leaving Sweden, I had some business I needed to attend to at the Swedish Embassy in Paris. I could only smile when I entered a quiet building, with no one else around, but was still directed to, yes, you guessed it, the little number machine!

Now when I'm back in the US, however, I often feel equally disoriented. The impact may even be compounded, because in the US no one thinks that I'm a foreigner; they just think I'm dumb.

Nothing creates more anxiety for me when I am in the US than trying to order at a fancy coffee establishment. The pace at which people are served is overwhelming. I dutifully devote my time in line to trying to figure out what I want, but I nearly have a panic attack when my turn comes up. All I can see on the board are sundry beverages consisting of whips, twists, and shots that all have names that end in "iatto" and come in multiple sizes that all mean big. Nothing resembles what I've come in for, so I meekly approach the overachieving barista and mumble my feeble order: I'd like the smallest darkest cup of brewed coffee you have, please. I leave it to them to figure out if that is a tall dark roast, no whip, room for milk, or what have you.

Then there's the debacle of writing the date. It took ages for me to adjust to the European system: day, month, year. I used an inordinate amount of mental energy in order to get this right as I trained my mind to switch to day, month, year. Day, month, year. Day, month, year. Day, month, year. Back in the US, I'm filling out a form and I instinctively write day, month, year, and I feel like a schoolgirl who has barely learned to write. The people at the bank or the library or wherever just kind of look at me with a bizarre sort of wonder, mingled with horror, trying to work out what kind of mental incapacity leads a grown woman to believe there are twenty-eight months in a year. Yet again, I walk away feeling the odd one out, wondering where in the world it is that I can truly land and feel at home. Disorientation. Alienation.

These sensations of alienation are disorienting and disruptive. They create anxiety, shake the ground on which we stand, rattle insecurities caged within our spirit, and give us the impression of being constantly on the outside looking in. We lack a sense of belonging, and this is indeed a very difficult place to live, let alone thrive. When I experience these feelings, I do so from a position of comfort and privilege. Most of the disorientation that I've experienced through my years of living abroad comes from lacking knowledge of how mundane things are done in a new place. I'm not trying to find a place to live, look for a job, or navigate a legal system so I can obtain permission to live in the new country in which I find myself. Even so, the pain of disorientation and alienation cuts quite deeply at times. I can only imagine what it's like for someone who is in a place of profound discomfort, operating out of a deep insecurity about their future, lacking financial and social resources, not knowing where in the world they will be able to rest their weary bodies, find nourishment for their souls, and provide for their loved ones. These are the feelings of disorientation and alienation that God wants Christians to recognize in the hurting people we encounter so that as a body of Christ we can offer comfort. We need to reach a deeper understanding of just how disorienting these experiences are for people in order to deepen our empathy enough to take action.

Name Your Alienation

Geography aside, I would venture to guess that we all have profound places in our lives where we retain that feeling of being on the outside, a sense of being a perpetual foreigner, where we feel alien. These are the areas that create deep insecurity within our spirit and can often prevent us from becoming all that God wants us to become. These are the things that chip away at our identity, cause us to wonder about who we are in this world, and wreak havoc with maintaining a positive self-image. Part of what helps us gain empathy for the outsider or the foreigner is to name those feelings and then choose to identify closely with others who share those feelings. It's important that all of us come to grips with a few key areas of our lives where we feel most like an alien; places that make us uncomfortable in our own skin; ways we feel that disorientation and alienation; areas that prevent us from feeling loved, celebrated, and embraced in the way that we know God wants us to be.

Fortunately, we are not alone in our feelings. Scripture is filled with stories of people who experienced displacement. An entire book of the Old Testament is dedicated to a mass exodus and reminds us of Moses and the Israelites who wandered in the wilderness for forty years.[2] Recall the previously mentioned stories of Abraham and Sarah, Joseph, Ruth and Naomi, and Jeremiah. Think of the Samaritan woman at the well who went to fetch water in the heat of the day to better hide from society.[3] Jesus, Mary and Joseph fled to a foreign land after being warned that their lives were in danger.[4] Scripture abounds with stories of people like us and our new neighbors, who describe the experience of disorientation while struggling through life when the bottom falls out. The ground beneath our feet, once firm, starts shaking, we lose our bearings and fall into a pit. Like the psalmist in Psalm 130, we yell from that pit, "From the depths of despair, O Lord, I call for your help. Hear my cry, O Lord. Pay attention to my prayer." Illness and other forms of personal distress, financial problems, and relational conflicts can make it seem as though God has abandoned us, or at least hidden for a while. We hurt. We question. We doubt. We may even despair of life itself. We are lost!

The wilderness is a primary metaphor for disorientation in the Bible, and this is fitting, for the word describes a state of losing direction or relationship with one's surroundings. A disoriented person is confused about where she is and where she may be going. The world becomes a barren, hostile place with no clear path to follow. The conditions are inhospitable. Shelter from the relentless heat is hard to find. We get thirsty. We may find ourselves joining the Psalmist once again in shouting: "O God, you are my God; I earnestly search for you. My soul thirsts for you; my whole body longs for you in this parched and weary land, where there is no water." (Psalm 63:1). When we are disoriented, we become desperate for a sense of security, for direction to return to our lives. We might even resist God's work of reorientation toward a new way forward in our desire for things to go back to making sense the way they once did. But the redemptive purpose of disorientation is not a blessed return to the status quo, nor is it skepticism, cynicism, or criticism, but the clearing away of the rubble, a removal

2. Exodus
3. John 4:4–42
4. Matthew 2:13-23

of things that block our vision of what God may be doing in our lives. In this way, our experiences of feeling like foreigners facing alienation from all that surrounds us, force us to rely upon the one thing that we know does not change: Jesus Christ, crucified and risen, alive and well in our midst.

It is not only our geographical position that makes us feel like aliens and strangers. We all have situations in our lives where we feel as though we are on the outside looking in. Some of these places may represent unfulfilled longings or places of deep pain and alienation. Others are areas of our lives where we feel unsettled, ill at ease, and certainly not at home. What I want to say is simply this: I believe with all my heart that God wants to use the places in our lives where we feel most alien, or most like a stranger, to draw us closer and to urge us on toward showing others the ministry of hospitality. God wants us to identify the areas of our life where we lack a sense of belonging in order to open up the doors to find our ultimate sense of belonging in being God's child, regardless of our earthly situation. It's where we feel off kilter that we grow in empathy towards those whose whole lives have been thrown off balance. In Deuteronomy we read: "For the Lord your God is God of gods and the Lord of lords. He is the great God, the mighty and awesome God, who shows no partiality and cannot be bribed. He ensures that the orphans and widows receive justice. He shows love to the foreigners living among you and gives them food and clothing" (Deuteronomy 10:17-18). What encouragement does this ancient text give us? First and foremost, it affirms that we are not abandoned by God in the places where we feel most alienated. In fact, it is precisely in these places where God can draw near to us in ways that our comfort zones never allow. When we are stripped of all that is comfortable and natural, we are forced to turn our eyes to that which lies beyond our reach. In these dark moments of disorientation and alienation we are forced to ponder the reality that God's ways are not our ways and to trust in his promises of a future filled with hope, in spite of all evidence to the contrary. God loves the alien and the stranger and promises to provide for them; I believe God wants us to be part of making that provision possible. That's why I think it's so important for us to identify in a deep, emotionally connected manner with the feelings of alienation that come with being the stranger.

Build Empathy

In order to fully understand what those on the outside of our society are feeling and living with, it's good for all of us to build empathy with them. You can gain a more visceral connection to the feelings and experiences that strangers and foreigners often bring to their complex situations even if you have never lived in a foreign country. Think about some of the non-geographical places in your life where you grapple with feelings of disorientation and alienation, or experience being on the outside looking in? Topping this list for me is the fact that I am not a mother. My husband and I tried for years to conceive a child, seeking medical attention, enduring one fruitless procedure after another. We pursued adoption on a number of fronts, but each time we felt we were making progress, something happened to thwart the process and we landed precisely where we began: childless.

As we grew older and emotionally exhausted by our pursuit of parenthood, we eventually faced and finally accepted the reality that we would never be parents. Even though we have not tried to get pregnant since 2001, this experience continues to shape me in profound ways that I am still sorting through. Many years later, and at this stage of my life, I am no longer hoping to get pregnant, but the permanent nature of our infertility can still cause searing pain and profound alienation at times. A deep sense of loss and shame emerges when I am with a group of women who speak of motherhood as the greatest gift a woman could ever know. I fear the scorn of those who think I have chosen to forgo motherhood because of selfish pursuits. I can almost hear them saying, "Well, if she hadn't been so focused on her career maybe she'd have found time to get pregnant."

Picture this horrific scene: Sunday morning, fifteen minutes before the service was to begin, a man who was a bit rough around the edges approached me and casually asked, "Don't want them or can't have them?" I said, "Excuse me?" And he repeated, "Don't want them or can't have them?" How in the world does one respond pastorally to such a crass and inappropriate comment? I wanted to punch him in the gut and scream in his face, "What's wrong with you? Do you not know that this is the most profoundly painful reality of my entire life? And yet you find it necessary to ask such cavalier and ridiculous questions, minutes before I have to lead you in worship?" Instead, I simply muttered, "Can't have them," and walked away, wounded, empty, profoundly alienated from all humanity in that small moment.

The scar of infertility is invisible. No one knows what to say when they ask if we have children, fully expecting me to say yes, of course, two and a half, and whip out photographs. In my gut I feel the need to help them feel better about their own awkwardness, shifting the subject or making a light joke. And then I am faced with a grim choice— to reveal the most intimate details of our journey through infertility to prove that we did not choose it but rather it chose us, or to simply let it go and instead allow them to default to whatever preconceived notions they may have about couples who do not have children. All of this is profoundly alienating for me and at times still brings on intense feelings of being forced apart from others—of not belonging. And yet, these feelings also force me to return to my identity in Christ as his beloved daughter, special and unique because God created me, valued not for being a mother, but for being God's child. This place of alienation is where God can truly work in my life, where I am fully disarmed and need to rely solely upon him.

Has my story stirred an empathetic response in your spirit? Is there something in your life that makes you feel like my infertility makes me feel? Name a place where you lack a true sense of belonging, where you feel like a stranger, the odd one out, an alien. Now imagine what it would be like to live with that sensation every minute of every day, never really knowing if you will belong ever again. The words of Matthew 25 to feed the hungry and welcome the stranger come into clearer focus when we think about the people who are struggling every single day with how to find a place to belong. By putting ourselves in their place, we understand the church's profound responsibility to offer hospitality to the stranger and create a special place of belonging for them. When we allow our empathy to deepen to that visceral level where we fully understand the pain of someone who stands outside, alienated, and disoriented, then and only then can we take willing and concrete steps toward caring for the strangers in our midst.

3

Understand with Compassion

IN THE LAST CHAPTER, in order to cultivate empathetic hearts, we considered where we ourselves might feel alienated from the broader society. The opportunity that we have to extend the ministry of hospitality to others who have been alienated by our societies is enormous and yet, we often miss the opportunity because we are afraid of others. I firmly believe that as we come to a clearer understanding of the difficult circumstances that people who are moving to foreign lands experience, our compassion for them will increase, and we will be better equipped to offer them the kindness that Jesus asks his followers to extend to others.

A Lost Passport

A few years back I had planned a trip to California to be with my folks. As is my custom, I was packing the night before and went to get my passport, but it wasn't snuggled safely in its special little place in Doug's dresser. Hmm. Where could it have gone? I tore up the house. No passport. I searched my church office, high and low. Nothing. I checked the refrigerator, the freezer. Finally I concluded that it must have been stolen or that I must have left it somewhere or thrown it away without realizing it. Ugh. Regardless, it was gone without a trace and I had to postpone my trip. I canceled my uninsured, non-refundable ticket. (Because really, why waste the money on travel insurance and refundable tickets when you know you'll never have a problem?) I was crawling into bed that night, trying to calm myself after hours of frantic, anxious searching, when another unsettling thought occurred to me. I was undocumented. No passport. Living in a foreign country. No way to leave the country and be sure I'd be allowed back in. No way to prove I could legally enter the US. My mom was sick and I wouldn't be able to see her for who knows how long because I was undocumented. I never ever thought that I would be in such a position.

I have to say, when I crawled into bed that night, I felt a little weird. I said to Doug, "There's no way for me to leave Sweden right now. I have no papers." When you live abroad, the ability to get to your loved ones in another country is of high value. Suddenly losing that ability was disorienting, unnerving. At Immanuel, hardly a week went by when we were not praying for someone to be granted "permission to stay." They had come as refugees with no chance of returning to their homeland and yet a permanent stay in their new country was still only a hope, an often elusive goal they themselves could do little to achieve. This is a deeply stressful place to be. I felt a tiny amount of that stress in the few hours I lived without a passport but I lived with it knowing that in due time I would be issued a new US passport, I had money to pay for the documents, late fees, phone calls, etc., and in the meantime had a job, a home, and stability. Plus I had legal status, just no proof of such. And yet it was still incredibly nerve-wracking. I gained an enormous amount of empathy for the people in our world living in those in-between places, sometimes for their whole lives.

My number one quest the next morning was acquiring a new passport. I had the added advantage of knowing someone who worked at the US Embassy, who spoke my language, and gave me a list of everything I needed to have before I arrived, including a police report and passport photos, which I took care of on my way to the embassy. Once there, they processed me quickly and told me I could pick up my new passport the following morning. Wow. I couldn't believe it. As soon as I left the embassy, I broke down in tears of relief. I had been more stressed out than I had even realized, and I was so grateful that the ordeal would be over in 24 hours. A dear friend had invited me to come to her home when I was done at the embassy so that she could give me a hug. That simple act of kindness and hospitality was a huge comfort. It said that I was going to be OK. I was loved. I was valued as a friend and person. All those convictions had been shaken when I realized that my passport was missing, and I was in need of the care and comfort of someone who offered me unconditional love without judgment.

Just think how acutely undocumented people must need these same assurances when securing a passport is not nearly as easy as it was for me. Take a moment to ponder how shaky the ground itself must seem for the person who cannot return to her homeland due to political tensions or safety issues. It doesn't take long to realize why simple and profound acts of hospitality are so important to displaced people and why the church should minister to these needs. Having experienced a small portion of the anxiety undocumented people must manage on a daily basis, I have also gained insight into the reality that no human being chooses to enter a journey of becoming an undocumented person in another country on a whim. There are deep and consequential reasons why people risk so much in seeking to move to another place, a place that often bears no resemblance to their native homeland. Those who are critical of people seeking to enter the US illegally sometimes have a jaded view of why people are seeking to re-locate. Somehow this notion that others want to take away our livelihood by coming in and stealing our country has gained steam across our globe. The reality is that most often, life in the place where they do have the papers to remain has somehow become untenable. No jobs. War. Disease. No future for them or their children. Put yourself in those circumstances and ask yourself what would drive you from your home to enter the enormously insecure world of migration, often through hostile conditions, only to be met with great resistance, racism, and misunderstanding. Living an undocumented life creates such enormous stress that it's quite hard for us who live with the power and privilege of place to understand why anyone would subject themselves to such peril. And yet they do, because life is just that challenging.

I still wonder why I felt so panicky and overwhelmed when my passport went missing. Nothing was life or death for me or my loved ones. Sure, the stressors of the moment were big, and the change of plans was disappointing, but I knew that I'd get another passport. I knew I wasn't going to be sent to jail. I knew that in the end, everything would be fine in a matter of due course. Everything that unnerved me was easily solved in a short period of time. I was able to resolve my lost passport issue from a place of great comfort, a privilege that I cannot forget. Others who are far less fortunate than I are sacrificing security and safety with the hope of providing security and safety for their family in the future. During my dilemma I felt a lot of things, but mostly sad and stupid. It was a tough mental adjustment from heading for a vacation in the sun to getting stuck working a few extra dark, cold days, but again, hardly life or death. This was a first world, person of privilege, problem. Of course, I wanted to spend some time with my parents as both of them were dealing with significant health issues at the time. I wanted to make every minute we had together count. But wouldn't this be true for any human being on the earth? And yet, not all of us have the luxury of traveling whenever and wherever we see fit. It is a privilege that I have the right to travel and the funding to do so.

In the midst of the craziness of not being able to find my passport, I lost my mind a bit. I allowed anxiety to grow large and I grew uncertain about my ability to make good choices. Fortunately, I was surrounded by the care and concern of good friends and a loving and patient husband. I had to keep reminding myself that this was not that dire of a situation, that I had options, that money was only money, that our lives were not going to be in tatters if we didn't get this worked out, and that even if I couldn't travel right then, I would be able to again in the near future. Even so, the stress that losing my passport and missing a flight caused me gave rise to a variety of thoughts and feelings, but ultimately the most predominant ended up being thankfulness. I am so grateful for the privileges I enjoy. And my empathy for those for whom life is not so easy grew one hundredfold over those forty-eight hours. Having resources, community, opportunities, and connections all make a huge difference in the way in which we enjoy life. When something trips up those of us with all of the above, it's stressful because it's disruptive, but it won't put our very lives at stake.

However, for others, who live in nations at war, with corrupt government systems, or without viable employment opportunities, undocumented refers to a way of life that carries more stress with it than I can comprehend. These dear people have the same human longings that I do for connection with their loved ones and homeland. And yet, they are banned from ever returning, usually because of circumstances well beyond their control. I had control over my circumstances and only logistics were keeping me from traveling when I lost my passport. I was going to get a new passport, travel to the US, spend time with my parents, etc. It was just a matter of time and money, both of which I had in abundance. But what I will always carry in my heart, in a special way, are those beloved people who live without proper papers in our world, knowing that the circumstances that landed them there are far more egregious than simply misplacing an important document. Additionally, the hope for resolution of their problems is much more complex than what I went through for all of forty-eight hours. My empathy for the feelings of those without proper documentation increased exponentially by experiencing in small part what it means to have plans thwarted for lack of papers.

While concerns about documented vs. undocumented and legal vs. illegal immigration are important, that is a different conversation than the one I am having with you today.[1] I am certain that God's command for us to care for the alien and stranger among us does not include the caveat: unless they are here illegally. It's certainly a difficult matter, but as the church, I believe our core calling is to hospitality, not to gatekeeping. Because God has a deep love for the needy and the disenfranchised, whoever they are and whatever the cause of their situation. God's is not a selective

---

1. For an in-depth study, see M. Daniel Carroll, Christians at the Border.

mercy. He cares for each human, because each one, as we have seen, is made in God's image. The most fundamental tenet of the Christian faith is that God loved the entire world so much that he sent his son Jesus to die for all of humanity.[2] The Bible also teaches that God is sovereignly involved in the movements of all peoples.[3] Today, this would mean that God is present in some way in the migrations we are witnessing worldwide. The book of Ruth offers us a rich perspective on these matters.

Learning from Boaz and Ruth

Perhaps you are familiar with the book of Ruth from the Old Testament. To summarize, Ruth ends up with her mother-in-law, Naomi, in desperate circumstances after a series of tragedies. They meet Boaz who allows them the chance to glean their fields. In Ruth 2 Boaz inquires about the young woman who has entered his field. His foreman informs him that she is the young woman from Moab who returned with Naomi. She wants to gather grain behind the harvesters as she is in great need. The foreman also mentions that she is a very hard worker. This gets Boaz's attention and so he approaches Ruth and offers her the opportunity to work in his fields, following his workers. He assures her that she will be protected, that none of his workers shall harm her. Boaz offers her water from his well and makes clear that he wants to care for her and provide for her needs. Ruth responds with humility and thanksgiving, wondering what she has done to deserve such kindness, especially since she is a foreigner. Boaz makes clear that he knows she is a foreigner, but that he is moved by Ruth having put herself in an even more difficult situation after the death of her husband in order to care for her mother-in-law. He lets her know that his compassion is a result of her compassion for Naomi that prompted her to leave her own family and homeland to live among complete strangers in a foreign land. Boaz, duly impressed with

2. John 3:16
3. Amos 9:7; cf. Acts 17:26-28

Ruth's strength of character, blesses her, saying "May the Lord, the God of Israel, under whose wings you have come to take refuge, reward you fully for what you have done" (Ruth 2:12). Ruth responds by expressing her deep gratitude for his kindness even though she is not one of his regular workers. Boaz's generosity toward Ruth doesn't stop there. He continues to make her life more comfortable by offering her food and bread from his abundance. He welcomes her to sit at the table with the workers and invites her to eat and drink as much as she would like. As Ruth returns to work in the field, Boaz issues an order to his young workers not only to allow her to take the leftovers from the harvest, but also to "accidentally on purpose" drop extra grain in the field for her to recover. He reminds them once again not to give her a hard time.

Several things strike me when I read about Ruth and her encounter with Boaz. Ruth never had to be a foreigner; she could have remained in her native land. She made this sacrifice out of compassion for Naomi, to accompany her mother-in-law through hardship. Boaz exhibits the kind of care that Christ asks of us in Matthew 25. These women are poor and he offers them work. They are hungry and he offers them food. They are thirsty and he provides them with drink. They are vulnerable and he promises them protection. He invites them to stay and work in his field rather than shooing them away and telling them to get their needs met elsewhere. Boaz invites Ruth to sit with his workers. He does not relegate her to a lesser seat at the table. He exhibits kindness toward Ruth, acknowledges that she has been through a very rough time, and marvels that she has chosen to forego bitterness in favor of caring for Naomi.

What if this story were to play out against the backdrop of today's vitriol against the immigrant? Perhaps it would go more like this: When Boaz sees Ruth, an uninvited foreigner, in his field, he instinctively worries that she is stealing from him, literally eating into his profits. He demands to see her papers. Unable to produce any, she tells Boaz her story, hoping that he will understand her difficult circumstances and that she has only come to this country and to this field to try to provide for herself and her grieving mother-in-law. Circumstances beyond her control prevent her from returning to her homeland. While Boaz finds her story moving, he doesn't want to be the one to help her. He's a busy man and has many people to manage. He doesn't need an illegal foreigner hanging around his field potentially stirring up trouble. Instead of the compassionate response we see in the biblical account, in today's world it is easy to imagine Boaz telling Ruth to leave and not come back. Maybe he is sorry that he can't give her work, but he is unable to overlook her status as an undocumented foreigner. Laws are laws and they must be obeyed. He sends her away with no food, no protection, no provision, no work. He does, however, promise to pray for her and in this way convince himself that he has fulfilled his calling as a Christian businessman.

It's an apalling alternate ending to this beautiful biblical story, but it is more true-to-life. This is our world's standard reaction to foreigners. We love the kindness that Boaz showed Ruth and Naomi, but sometimes we have a hard time seeing how we can be the ones to offer that kindness. Our own prejudices get in the way of our ability to minister to those in deep need. Both Boaz and Ruth model ways in which Christ calls us to care for those who are vulnerable. Ruth's incredibly selfless decision to care for Naomi in the midst of great hardship inspires and moves us to want to live more sacrificially. Boaz's unrelenting kindness and offer of protection as a person with power and privilege gives us insight into how to truly care for a foreigner or stranger in our midst. No matter what your politics, it's clear that the biblical message is to be more like Boaz.

Members of God's Family

Boaz broke societal barriers through his care for Ruth and Naomi. He embraces them as family rather than dismissing them as lowly foreigners. The book of Ephesians delves into this stunning notion of old barriers coming down between people.

> Don't forget that you Gentiles used to be outsiders. You were called "uncircumcised heathens" by the Jews, who were proud of their circumcision, even though it affected only their bodies and not their hearts. In those days you were living apart from Christ. You were excluded from citizenship among the people of Israel, and you did not know the covenant promises God had made to them. You lived in this world without God and without hope. But now you have been united with Christ Jesus. Once you were far away from God, but now you have been brought near to him through the blood of Christ. (Ephesians 2:11-13)

The passage goes on to explain that Jesus is now our peace, having destroyed the dividing wall of hostility. One of the key verses that speaks to our identity as children of God through Christ's actions follows.

> So now you Gentiles are no longer strangers and foreigners. You are citizens along with all of God's holy people. You are members of God's family. Together, we are his house, built on the foundation of the apostles and the prophets. And the cornerstone is Christ Jesus himself (Ephesians 2:19-20).

Clearly, in Christ, the earthly dividing lines of who's in and who's out have been redrawn and the centering point of our citizenship is in Christ. If we begin to see all people as members of God's family, instead of defining them by their social status or documentation, it helps us to cultivate empathy for those who are longing to find a place of belonging in a hostile environment. Shouldn't the church be that soft place to land, that place of acceptance and care, where all are invited into the household of God? What then should we do in order to live into our calling to the ministry of hospitality, especially to the foreigner and outsider? Begin to see the person, not the status or circumstances. We need to be willing to embrace all people as children of God and as such, treat them as full members of the family of God.

Seeing with the eyes of Christ

The great German theologian Dietrich Bonhoeffer said, "We must see things differently, see people differently. No longer does the Christian see persons nakedly, but through the eyes of Christ."[4] As Christ followers, we should be willing to set aside our own comfort in order to provide comfort for one another because Christ has done that for us. It's often hard to interact with people who are different than we are. It happens that people who live on the fringe, strangers and foreigners, are, at times, dirty or unkempt. Sometimes they don't speak our language, literally or figuratively. They have different customs, different values. Part of showing real hospitality to others is not requiring them to become like us in order to fit in. It demands that we open ourselves up to another way of doing and being that accommodates the other. Being truly receptive is far more costly than staying the same and asking other people to do all the work of adapting to us. Think about that place of alienation that you considered earlier—what makes you feel most cared for in that circumstance? Being seen and accepted just as you are? Being shown kindness and compassion? Being shown empathy? Being welcomed into a place you could be yourself and still belong? Should we not be willing to do the same for others?

The Church as the Place to Belong

Our ministry in international churches in Europe for the past twenty years was centered around welcoming the stranger. Was it easy? Not always. Was it chaotic? Most of the time. Was it the most fun and the deepest joy we've ever experienced? Absolutely. The church should be the place where the ostracized of society find a place of belonging. In order to do that, however, the church needs to fight against becoming a closed circle. That is easier and decidedly more comfortable, but as Christ-followers we need to push ourselves to remain open to the new family members that

---

4. Bonhoeffer, The Cost of Discipleship, p. 257.

the Lord wants to add to our fellowship.[5] I am sure that most of us have been on the receiving end of someone's generous hospitality. I am confident that we have all been changed by the gracious action exhibited towards us when we needed that warm welcome. I am also confident that people will more clearly see Jesus through unexpected acts of hospitality. With this in mind, every church should cultivate a desire to be a welcoming community, taking intentional steps towards making sure the doors are wide open to all who wish to enter.

The Greek word for hospitality that is used in the New Testament is *philoxenos* . . . from the roots *philo*, which means brotherly love, and *xenos*, which means stranger . . . love for the stranger. This is the very opposite of xenophobia . . . which is *xeno* (stranger) and *phobia* (fear) . . . fear of the stranger. Encountering the stranger is something we will continue to do in a world that is on the move; it is our choice to either love or fear the stranger. If we truly believe in the ministry of hospitality, then we need to work at embracing *philoxenos* as a core value in our church.

As the Christian church, we have such an amazing opportunity to show the love of Jesus to so many people who are ready and eager to encounter the Lord's kindness. The international church has often been the place where strangers and foreigners find a profound sense of belonging. In the next chapter I'll share some stories of people who found themselves surrounded by the love of Christ in their new homelands.

---

5. Acts 2:47

4

Realize Who Moves

THERE ARE COUNTLESS REASONS why a person might find herself a stranger in a strange land. Some people move of their own free will, hoping for wider cultural experiences or an interesting adventure abroad; others are asked to move for their jobs; while some are forced to move to another situation out of fear for their lives. Some move hoping to provide a better future for themselves or for their children. What is true about those who move, with or without proper documentation, is that in their core being they want what all of us want—a brighter future for their kids, a chance to make an honest living, and escape from the dangers of war, poverty, and disease. We need to rid ourselves of the notion that immigrants are moving to other lands to take something away from the native population. It's a distortion of the truth to believe that most people who move from their homelands to another land are doing so for inherently evil reasons. These myths are often stoked by a volatile political climate that upholds nationalism as the highest ideal.

Even for people who move with paperwork in order, with the assistance of a company and financial backing, the moves are hard. When we first moved to Sweden, we had jobs, an apartment waiting for us, and the resources of the church which helped us open a bank account, set up our phone, TV, and internet connections, find doctors when necessary, navigate the public transportation system, get language lessons, and begin to understand how to grocery shop. Even so, I was lonely. I missed my former job. I missed my friends. Work was new and I was still trying to figure out what the day in, day out would look like. I was longing for the US. So when Doug and I sat down to breakfast one morning and he reeled off all of the things he was going to do that day and then finally asked me what I was going to do, I dryly replied, "I'm looking at airfares to Chicago." A stunned silence followed.

My point is this: whether you are walking thousands of miles with only the clothes on your back, hoping to escape an untenable situation in the place where you were born, or you have moved with the backing of a corporation, the same human longings remain: Finding community. Understanding your place. Discovering a meaningful livelihood. It's an exciting prospect to believe that the church could be the mechanism through which so many of these longings are satisfied. What follows are real-life scenarios of people I know who, after seeking out the fellowship of international churches in their new homelands, discovered community and comfort that had been previously missing.[1]

Leah and Erik

Leah is a brilliant scientist who was born in Ghana and raised in England. Her father was a Presbyterian pastor, and he ended up pastoring a church in London. Upon completion of her Ph.D., Leah had an opportunity to move to Ethiopia to work at a clinic for people with leprosy. There she met Erik, an equally brilliant medical doctor from Sweden. They fell in love and prepared to move to Stockholm together. Life was hard for Leah upon arrival in Sweden. Even though she had landed a job with the prestigious Karolinska Institute in Stockholm, people assumed from her dark skin that Leah was a refugee, and therefore unemployed and unskilled. Living in the shadow of her well-known and respected Swedish

---

1. The names have been changed.

husband eventually tore their marriage apart. But as love would have it, they decided that life together was much better than life apart. They rejoined their lives with a new understanding of how important it was for Leah to forge her own identity in their "new to her" homeland. Part of gaining a stronger identity for her was finding her own place of belonging and acceptance at Immanuel International. Leah could commiserate with the struggles other foreigners were having and find joy in meeting other internationals. The strength of the international Christian community also allowed Erik to encounter a very different style of church life than he had experienced in his Swedish upbringing. Erik wasn't as well-known in the foreign community, so he got to be just another guy in the fellowship, and it proved to be an effective and important place for him to deepen his own faith. The church has become a central place of comfort, joy, and peace for both Leah and Erik as they have recommitted to their life together.

Michael and Erica

Michael showed up at a Tuesday night bible study before he made the permanent move to Stockholm with his family. He was testing the waters of the city as he prepared to move his wife and three children from the US to Stockholm. His wife, Erica, is Swiss while Michael is American. To further complicate the cultural identity of their family, all three of their children were born in England. This truly international family had a lot going on in their lives when Michael took a new job with a European company based in Stockholm. Their oldest had graduated from high school in the US but the two youngest were quite devastated to have their American life torn away from them. Living closer to the Swiss side of the family brought them all a deep sense of joy but it was a difficult move after eight years of living in a tightly knit community in the US. The church welcomed them with open arms and being a family with a husband and wife from two different countries was more normative than odd at Immanuel International. The ever-dreaded question, "Where are you from?" was not asked with the same kind of scrutiny the children had come to loathe.

They quickly made Immanuel International their church home. Michael was thrilled to find a place where the English language was spoken and Erica, while fluent in English, was equally as thrilled to meet other German speakers. The church became the place where every aspect of their lives and backgrounds could be celebrated and given expression. It was helpful to find other couples and families who came from different cultures and could resonate with the joys and challenges of such.

Dana

Having completed her Ph.D. in biology, Dana was a rising young scientist when she landed a postdoc position at the Karolinska Institute in Stockholm. While raised in the Christian faith, she had become disillusioned by the church as an organization. She found Immanuel International through a friend and began attending church regularly. She got connected to the young adult group and formed a strong circle of friendships with other young professionals, some in her related field. It was refreshing for her to find a church where her background in science wasn't seen as being in conflict with her faith. As a single woman living abroad, she was grateful for the connections with people who shared her faith that would have otherwise been lacking in her life in Stockholm. Friendships functioned like family especially during those lonely holiday times when she was separated from her family of origin.

Peter and Katarina

Peter came from Zimbabwe and Katarina from Ukraine. They had faced much ugliness in their life together from people who didn't like that they were also a mixed-race couple. Katarina had little background in Christianity, having been raised in a communist country, but found the family of faith at Immanuel International a place of safety and warmth. After years of living in Stockholm, establishing Peter's career as an economist, they were finally going to fulfill their lifelong dream of moving back to live out their golden years on their property in Zimbabwe. But a collapsing economy in Zimbabwe and Peter's desire to fight for the people by joining the Movement for Democratic Change resulted in Peter's arrest. Katarina was able to get out and return to Sweden, but Peter was detained, and his future was uncertain. The prayers of the church and the practical support (housing, loans, a car) that Katarina received from Immanuel International sustained them both while many from the church nervously awaited and prayed for Peter's release from prison. Finally, through the compassion of a guard who had mercy on him, Peter escaped and returned to Sweden. The church was a pivotal source of both practical and moral support for this couple during Peter's imprisonment and also after his return to Swedish soil.

Rachel

Rachel, an American, was married to an Indian man whose job had landed them in Stockholm. Their marriage was challenging, and they had two small boys. Rachel was navigating a lonely road, knowing that her spouse was uninterested in spiritual matters and concerned that her marriage was going to fail. She wanted her boys to be surrounded by a Christian community and needed the support of a larger church family. She found Immanuel International and shortly thereafter set up an appointment with me. My first meeting with Rachel was memorable. I sensed that we both knew we'd become friends of the heart, sharing the pain and joy of life. Her marriage did end but by that time the church had truly become her nuclear family. She was able to create a life and a home for her and her boys while finding friendships and support through the international community.

Tom and Lisa

Tom and Lisa were a young couple from the United States, newly married, when Tom's job transferred him to Stockholm. Tom had an adventuring spirit but the move was a bit of a stretch for Lisa. She was a marriage and family therapist, and finding meaningful work was going to be difficult for her. Additionally, as a young married couple, they knew that the fellowship and accountability of a church community was going to be key for their continued growth. I vividly remember their first Sunday at Immanuel International. I saw two young people wander into the sanctuary, searching for a seat, looking a little bit timid. I approached them after the service, introduced myself and welcomed them. Their search for a church ended that day. They dug into life at Immanuel International, Lisa finding joy and support in the women's bible study group, while Tom used his leadership gifts leading the young adult bible study. The years went by. They had their first child in Stockholm. In fact, we drove them to the hospital at 2:30 in the morning when Lisa went into labor with their first child. Tom's job had him traveling a fair amount and the church community surrounded Lisa with the company she needed to avert the deep loneliness she sometimes experienced having a spouse who was often on the road. Eventually, Lisa was even hired by the church to provide counseling to those with a need for therapy in English. God more than fulfilled their prayer for a church where they could grow and learn and use their gifts as a young married couple.

Paige

Paige had received an appointment from the British government to work in the United Kingdom embassy in Stockholm. Moving abroad as a young single woman was both exciting and daunting. She found her way to Immanuel International and showed an interest in getting involved. She shared her musical gifts with the worship team, she opened her home for the young adult Bible study group, she volunteered as a youth leader. She joined the board and after one year, began to serve as chair. We often joked that Paige put in more hours as a volunteer than some staff members! Through the years, as her pastors, we began to see that she had gifts for ministry that needed to be pursued. We challenged her to begin thinking about obtaining a theological education. We commissioned her one Sunday morning as she was leaving Sweden for seminary studies in the US. Seeds of her call were planted, watered, and nurtured through her ministry at Immanuel.

Petras and Senait

Petras and Senait were refugees from Eritrea. The war between Ethiopia and Eritrea had made it impossible for them to consider staying in Eritrea. There was no future livelihood for either of them. They met and married in Stockholm and found International International where they could nurture their faith, gain support for their young marriage, and raise their three children in a Christian environment. They valued all their relationships with others in the international community, but the church was also a gathering spot for other Eritreans, and this unique source of support and continued connection with their homeland brought great comfort to them both. Life wasn't always easy for them, as stable employment sometimes eluded them, but the church was a focal point in their lives and a constant source of encouragement.

Hamza and Benazir

Hamza showed up at the church one day and my husband met with him. Forced out of Pakistan for fear of his life, Hamza had left a wife and four children behind. He was seeking political asylum and longed to bring his family to Sweden where better educational and occupational opportunities existed for his three daughters and newborn son. It took years for him to finally obtain permission to stay and subsequently bring his family over. What a day it was when several folks from Immanuel International surrounded this dear man as he watched his family come through customs, re-united after four long years. Hamza had become active in the church upon his arrival, and the entire family's faithful ministry was foundational in the years that followed. The three girls have now graduated from university and the son graduated from high school this year. Hamza initially struggled to find meaningful work but Benazir, his wife, was able to land a job teaching in a nearby school. Through their incredible hospitality, many were able to enjoy the fruit of their table and Hamza now has a catering business that has provided meaningful and fruitful employment. I can think of no other family who embodies the notion of hospitality more than Hamza and Benazir. Even when their own needs were great, and money wasn't always plentiful, they found a way to invite guest after guest into their home.

Justin and Rose

Justin and Rose moved to Stockholm from England, then moved back to England, then moved back to Stockholm, all for jobs that Justin had landed. All three of their children were born in Sweden. As a musician, Justin's career took off in Sweden, but Rose struggled at times to know how to handle their new life in a different country. Justin became fluent in Swedish, but going to church where the English language was spoken was a better place for the entire family to grow in their faith. Despite their Anglican background, they found the international church to be a better fit for them. They enjoyed the broad diversity, more relaxed worship style, and connection to the Swedish congregation that Immanuel International offered. A job took them back to England for a season, but they felt the pull of Stockholm once again and found themselves back on Swedish soil after a few years in their home country. Their oldest child, Aaron, was now in university but spent summers in Stockholm as an intern in the church working with children and youth. He subsequently returned to Stockholm after university with his English wife, Zoey. Aaron and Zoey were later hired as the worship leaders/sound technicians at the church. Justin and Rose's two daughters spent their formative years in Stockholm. After university studies in England, both have returned to careers in Sweden. Justin and Rose were deeply involved in the life of the church, both with the international ministry but also on the Board of Directors of the entire church and other Swedish language committees. Their involvement proved invaluable in helping Immanuel International navigate the often difficult road of integrating with the Swedish church.

Keza

Keza was a single woman coming to Sweden as a refugee out of Rwanda. She was denied refugee status, however, and was forced to live illegally while pursuing her case for staying in Sweden. Life was not easy during this in-between time. A loophole in the Swedish system made it easier for her to gain permission to stay if she had a child. She got pregnant and gave birth to a beautiful baby girl. Shortly thereafter she married her Kenyan husband and together they were able to pursue a pathway for legally staying in Sweden. Initially nervous about how her church community, who had loved and supported her so deeply, would react to her out-of-wedlock pregnancy, she was overwhelmed at the continued embrace the community showed her. The day that her child was baptized nearly the entire church had tears streaming down their faces, rejoicing for the gift of this cherished child. Keza named her Precious, a perfect reflection of how the congregation felt about both Keza and her daughter.

Ify and Hakeem

Ify and Hakeem came from Nigeria seeking a better life in Sweden. They had a two-year-old son named Philip. They were not living in Sweden legally but were in the process of seeking permission to stay. Life was lonely, but the church gave them friends that were like family. Ify got pregnant with their second and when he was born with Down's Syndrome, it shattered their world. They were unfamiliar with Down's Syndrome and had no idea what it meant for them. Fearing that their baby was somehow cursed, my initial visit with Ify calmed her fears and helped her see that this child was special. The church came around them; the baby would grow up surrounded by love, affirmed for who he was, a precious child of God. The day we baptized him, Ify cried and cried, tears of joy as she issued forth joyous and heartfelt hallelujahs for what God had done in their lives. The continued care and support from the church community helped them come to grips with having a special needs child and the love poured out on all of them has been transformative in helping them accept their son as a gracious gift from God.

Marisol and Anders

As a young Filipina, Marisol had married an older Swedish man and they landed in Stockholm to start their life together. Marisol gave birth to a son and she longed to raise him in the Christian church. Her husband, Johan, was not a believer nor was he interested in the church, so Marisol's journey to church with her son was one she traveled alone. Marisol's presence in my life was immeasurably valuable. I always said that when I was discouraged in ministry, all I had to do was to think of Marisol, and I was immediately inspired to carry on. She embodied joy and unrelenting faith in Christ. Everyone could see it. Everyone but her husband, that is. Johan was a bad man, a gambler who was violent with Marisol, but she spent years with him, believing that God would not want her to divorce. We were finally able to help her understand that Johan had already broken his marriage vows and that for her safety and that of her son, God would be OK with her leaving. Years later, she met a gentle soul at Immanuel International, and the two of them fell deeply in love. Doug and I were privileged to marry them a few months later. Anders and Marisol are a beautiful couple who exude the love of Christ in all aspects of their lives. They are also among the most hospitable people I've ever met, opening wide the doors of their home to welcome all who need a place of comfort.

Titus

Titus showed up at church one Sunday with a vague story of how he had found his way to Stockholm from Liberia. It seemed apparent that he did not have the proper paperwork to stay in Sweden and was scrambling to figure out how to get permission to stay. But he was a faithful participant in our church, eager to serve and help out wherever he could. However, attempts to get him to fill out the forms which would allow us to contact him, connect him to our mailing list, and follow up on things never yielded a satisfactory result. It took me way too long to realize that he wasn't filling out the paperwork because he was illiterate. Titus couldn't read or write much beyond his name. It opened my eyes to the reality of how little opportunity some people have in this life to gain the basic skills they need to function well in an ordered society. I give Titus a lot of credit. He eventually found the pathway to staying in Sweden and obtained employment and the means to build a life in Stockholm.

Refugees

I took a trip to Egypt recently. While there I learned a bit about the refugees who are pouring into Cairo from Syria. These people come to Cairo with few or no resources. They do not speak the language. They often have children accompanying them. They are forced to wander around the city looking for help, hoping to find a way to provide shelter and food for themselves and their family. They are willing to work if they can find a job. Their lives are hard. They are on the move because their homeland is a hostile war zone and they fear for their lives and the lives of their children. Why would anyone subject themselves to such hardship if they didn't believe that a safer, better life awaited them? Refugees and vulnerable migrants are not seeking to steal from the country they are attempting to enter. They, like you and me, only want a chance at a better, safer life for them and their families. They deserve to be greeted with compassion and care, not suspicion, distrust, and hostility.

Thankfully, St. Andrews United Church of Cairo, an international church, offers help for refugees through their St. Andrew's Refugee center (StARS). Their purpose is twofold: to provide high-quality services meeting unaddressed needs of refugees, and to provide a safe and inclusive space for displaced people to come together as a community. God's desire to see his people care for the foreigner and the stranger is lived out through this ministry. Imagine the impact of more churches adopting a similar vision for caring for the most vulnerable in our world. St. Andrews offers us a great model for how we can become the hands and feet of Jesus seeking to care for people who feel forced to leave their homeland. Opportunities to provide legal assistance, teach English and professional development courses, care for children, especially those who have been separated from their parents, and assist people with finding housing are a few of the services available through StARS. Visit their website for more information.[2]

I could tell you countless other stories of people from India, China, the Philippines, Germany, Rwanda, Nigeria, Kenya, Indonesia, the Netherlands, the United Kingdom, South Africa, Canada, the United States, France, Mexico, Honduras, Guatemala, Syria, Iraq and so many other beautiful places in our world who, for one reason or another, find themselves on the move. In all honesty, there are details embedded within each story that could serve as temptations not to welcome someone. Many who came through our door were undocumented, living in Sweden illegally but trying to figure out how to make it. Some came from countries where life was a mess, unemployment was exploding, or the infrastructure was breaking down along with the local economy collapsing making it difficult for anyone to make an honest living. But difficult as the circumstances were, the country wasn't listed as a nation

2. http://stars-egypt.org/

where someone leaving could be given refugee status and so the choice for people was to stay in their homeland and try to scrape together an existence that might be fruitful but was more likely to frustrate, or to risk everything and head to a place where they might improve their lot. Others made very poor choices and, perhaps in some people's minds, wouldn't deserve help because they created the messy circumstances that they now had to deal with. No matter the circumstances of their arrival, we made a choice to welcome people. We provided physical and practical aid when possible, but at the very least, we represented one place they could count on being accepted and made to feel that they belonged.

I have shared here just a smattering of the broad diversity of circumstances that result in people living as strangers in a strange land. It may be easy to scan the list and envision your community welcoming "those types of people" as well, but wouldn't that imply that there are other "types of people" in different circumstances who would be less welcome? When we lived in Stockholm, on more than one occasion, someone told us that we were "the right kind" of immigrant. I'm sure their intent in saying this was to make me feel more welcome, but I actually found it disturbing and offensive. I regret that I didn't have the courage to reply that my church was full of the "wrong kind" immigrants and they were magnificent human beings, contributing to society, working hard, wanting the same beautiful life that most locals enjoyed. Each person I mentioned here, made a place for themselves in the new homeland, in large measure because of the hospitality and encouragement of the international church, and went on to have a significant ministry at Immanuel International. Many served on the international church council and some served on the Board of Directors for the whole church. All volunteered in key ministry positions on Sundays, including singing in the choir, teaching Sunday School, ushering, serving during the fellowship hour that followed our worship service, playing on the worship team, helping with sound or technical needs, and perhaps most significantly, staffing our welcome table. They all caught the vision keeping the doors open wide for the next person who was as starved for community as they had once been. Additionally, those mentioned above formed a core of people who exhibited hospitality gifts more faithfully than any other people I've met. We would have missed out on a treasure trove of giftedness had we not welcomed these folks into our community. What they have given back to church far surpasses anything that we might have given to them. And that is another reason why it shouldn't matter to the church why a person is on the move. It should only matter that a person who has moved is likely lacking community, friendship, support, and a sense of belonging because the church has a unique and wonderful opportunity to provide all of these things. So very often, because these folks bear the memory of what it means to be the stranger, they themselves become the most generous with their time and exude hospitality to those in need of a soft place to land during hard transitions.

Mark my words, no matter how long someone has been in a "new" homeland, the longing for one's country of origin never goes away. It's important to note that in most cases, all things being equal, most people would rather live in their homeland than immigrate to another country. It is often unjust and dangerous circumstances that drive people to another place. When we encounter people living with these circumstances, we should never forget the pain and sacrifice that comes along with these moves if we want to minister to those in need of God's love and Christ's compassion. Hearing the stories of why people have landed in a new situation helps us to embrace and not judge. Our job in the church is to provide hospitality and comfort to those who need it the most, not to pick and choose who is worthy of our attention and care.

5

Grasp the Great Opportunity

PERSONAL NARRATIVES HELP US see the people and not just the issue. They act as a catalyst that helps move our churches toward becoming the welcoming place that strangers and foreigners need, but developing greater understanding of those who are on the move and why is only part of the equation for becoming a more welcoming church. A desire to live out the gospel by welcoming strangers mobilizes our faith communities to love others with the love of Christ.

Landing in a new place as a stranger or foreigner, no matter the reason, carries with it a lot of emotions and insecurities. The feelings are heightened if you have yet to master the native language. Even if plenty of people around you speak a language that you understand and can converse in, it is overwhelming to start from scratch in a new place.

In asking a variety of people about the difficulties of making a new place home, I noticed several overarching themes emerging. Feelings associated with being lost and isolated were common. Homesickness for the places and loved ones they left behind. Missing the feeling that they were in control of their lives. Small things become big things; knowing where to go to find something, how to get to work without getting lost. Navigating the grocery store can suck down an entire day's energy. The sadness of watching their children struggle to make new friends and suffer through their own feelings of loneliness and longing. Being new is tough. It's hard not knowing anyone. People rarely felt that they truly fit in, which intensified the loneliness and isolation.

These reflections all point to one central tenet: no matter our situation in life, one of our deepest longings is to belong. There are so many places where a stranger doesn't enjoy this sense that if the church can be the place where anyone can belong, well, it follows that people will be moved to stay after visiting. And isn't that what Christ's followers should want the church to be: a place where people long to come? Once these "strangers" found a church home in their new situation, their comments about their new place of residence changed. People experienced fitting in at church even when they felt out of step with the world around them almost everywhere else; the church became the one place that helped people feel less alone. Most found navigating a new society exhausting and were grateful that at church they didn't feel like a foreigner all the time, or at least not the only foreigner. Even this brought a measure of comfort and relief. The church has great gifts to offer our newest neighbors—an ability to be themselves. The opportunity to stay spiritually vital in the midst of other stressful situations. Life often felt one-dimensional before finding a church home; the church helped people feel more well-rounded. The church gave people relationships outside of their jobs and provided space for the non-working spouse to build relationships and make connections. People realized that when they had a need, it was the church folks who they called and not their work colleagues.

For strangers and foreigners, the church is often the place where relationships that take on the qualities of family emerge, especially when one's blood family is far away and opportunities to visit are few or even non-existent. Parents with small kids often expressed the importance of connecting with others outside of the home. The "trailing spouse," uprooted and relocated as an afterthought to the work assignment that brought them to a new place, is left alone to figure out school, medical needs, shopping, transportation, etc. while the working spouse often has it a bit easier given that their daily work routines remain a big chunk of their lives. After talking with a family who had moved for the man's job, the man said to me, "The kids are doing well in school; I just work, so it doesn't matter whether I'm in New York or London; but my wife is suffering the most. She's the one who has had to rebuild her social networks and figure out the day-to-day for us all." Many people mentioned finding an affinity group really helped them adjust. Connecting with others who share a similar interest or life situation is helpful not only for problem solving but also in being reminded you are not alone in all this. Small groups provide opportunities to study the bible while building deeper relationships. Young adult groups provide connections that singles often lack. A choir gives people the chance to connect with others who share a similar love of music and singing. Youth groups help kids cross over boundaries through planned socials where, hopefully, being stigmatized for being new or different is minimized by caring adults. The main driver for people wanting to find an affinity group to join is that they need and want to reduce the feeling that they are alone. The church can and should be the place that provides healing for these longings.

Through the years I have received many kind notes, (granted, a few ugly ones too, but those are not germane to this conversation), about how meaningful the ministries that we've been a part of have been in people's lives. I keep two of these notes near at hand, and read them often, as they have meant so much to me. The first, from a Japanese couple who were in Stockholm for the husband's business was written in a Christmas card one year. "Thank you for inviting us to your home. We thank God that our pastors are tenderhearted for the foreigners like us." The second came from a young woman involved in our young adult ministry in Paris. It was given to us at our farewell party. "I thank you for putting so much effort into welcoming people. We often don't know what people's stories are. This welcome has meant a lot to me." I mention these meaningful tokens of kindness given to us not to flaunt our personal ministries, but rather to illuminate the depth of joy people experience when they are welcomed. These came from people we were not particularly close to but even so, they were moved by the spirit of hospitality.

Simply by cultivating an ethos of welcome for people, no matter their story, the church has a huge opportunity to reveal the love of God in Christ. That is why I feel that in so many ways, it should be a no-brainer for the church to meet people where they are, to open wide their doors for people who are searching and longing for a place to belong. The longing in people's hearts to find a community of faith is often very deep, so let's not disappoint people by not being welcoming! When people are lonely and longing for connection, they are open and vulnerable, and the church has such an amazing opportunity to be the place that begins to soothe those feelings of isolation and alienation. Being part of the solution that helps foreigners find their way into their new homelands instead of being part of the hostility that resents newcomers coming in and "messing with our traditions" and supposedly creating a burden on our society is an opportunity that the church cannot afford to miss. It's important to grasp the chance we have to reach people who are hungry for love and acceptance. When we do, we honor God and give people a glimpse of Christ's unconditional love. But it can be costly and that is why we struggle sometimes to live into being a truly welcoming church.

6

Count the Costs

MOST CHURCHES WANT TO be welcoming, at least in theory. But it seems somewhat obvious that if churches are not growing, then new people are not being welcomed. One of the realities of being a welcoming church is that you must commit to be a changing church, and that is often very hard. People don't like change. People resist change. But it's not fair to simply say to others that you want them to come and be a part of your community but expect that they will do all the changing. The subculture of your church must reflect an openness to new people and that includes welcoming strangers and foreigners. This means that people must be flexible and open to new experiences. Sometimes we get it wrong and think that reducing discomfort is the only solution. It isn't. Coping with discomfort is what will allow an openness to be sustained over the long haul. So alongside of working at creating a culture of openness, there must be a willingness on the part of the leadership to help people cope with their discomfort. Naming our discomfort helps us to gain dominion over it. It's okay to feel discomfort. It's not okay for that discomfort to keep you from doing important, meaningful ministry.

Keep Learning

Being part of a diverse community means you will always be on a learning curve! There will always be something you need to understand better. There will always be a differing point of view that deserves to be considered. There will often be misunderstandings that will require energy to get ironed out. Remember Hamza from the previous chapter? The one I called one of the most hospitable people I've ever met? Well, it took some time for me to understand the way in which he wanted people to feel welcome in his home. Hamza's manner of inviting us to an event in his home was to get very close to my face and to demand that we come to his house! He'd say, "Jodi, on the 7th of July you will come to my house for my son's birthday party." Initially I bristled at this. My American response was to think (or rather, shout in my head), "You will not tell me what to do. I will come to your house if I want to and not just because you are demanding it." I have to chuckle a bit now because if I had stubbornly refused to go to his house due to not liking the way in which he invited me, I would have missed out on some of the most amazing gatherings that I've ever had the privilege to be part of. In Hamza's mind, the more forceful the invitation, the more deeply he wanted me to come. It was his way of showing me how much it would mean to him if I would come. What first appeared to be a strong command in my mind, eventually came to be seen as an act of love. What sounded demanding and bossy in my ears was actually his deep desire to state how gladdened he would be if I could come and grace his home with my presence.

In order to grow, we have to stay open to new ways of doing and being and, truth be told, this can be exhausting. A commitment to continuing to be open is tiring. It takes a lot of effort to keep reaching out, reaching new people, grafting newcomers into your existing structure. But it is an effort that is buoyed by the return on the investment! Helping people see the bright side of being open is a key aspect of continuing to grow into the open and diverse church we should all be longing to be. Yes, new situations are scary, but they can also be incredibly rewarding. What if we diverted some of that fear that makes us overly protective of the way things are toward a healthy concern for what we will miss out on if we wall off our communities?

Care for the Fatigued

Care must also be given to long-term members for whom a fatigue factor may set in. It's hard to keep building new relationships, staying open to new folks coming in, and spending energy getting to know them while grafting them into your community. Figuring out ways to both nurture and sustain your long-term members while cultivating a climate of openness is hard to do but it is a worthy pursuit. Acknowledging that it takes courage and strength to stay open is important. Naming the more permanent community's sense of perpetual loss as other people come and go helps to provide support for those in danger of becoming too weary of goodbyes to say hello to anyone new.

In the midst of seeking to build intercultural bridges between people with differing backgrounds, it's also important to respect and encourage intracultural spaces, making time for people from similar cultures to get together without having to worry about integrating. Constantly overriding our cultural defaults puts a strain on the system; spaces where we can be with others from our background, speak our own language, and reference our own cultural quirks without worrying about offending or leaving someone out function as release valves from the tension. Time to be with others like ourselves actually increases our ability to be more open to change and diversity at other times.

Allowing people to have rest from leadership is also key. No matter how gifted someone may be, burnout is real for everyone. Sometimes a short break is in order. Other times a longer break will be necessary. Rest leads to restoration, which leads to being empowered for ministry. We must allow people opportunities to refuel along the way. Our dependence on one another is interwoven into our desire to be a welcoming and open community.

Everyone Gives up Something

Everyone must be willing to give up something that is important to them in order to make room for something different that is important to someone else. At Immanuel International, we used to say to all newcomers, no one gets it their way all the time, but everyone gets it their way some of the time. Insisting on your point of view or your preferences will never allow your community to grow and develop. As people exhibit an openness to something different, something new and meaningful emerges. Not always, but often. There were times when we'd sing a song or do something in our service that I really didn't like. I'd mention it to Doug and he'd say, "I know. I don't really like it either, but there's nothing theologically flawed about it and lots of people have expressed how much they do enjoy it. So, we incorporate it once in a while." See, even the pastor doesn't always love everything that takes place in a worship service! It takes effort to cultivate a spirit of openness to new experiences. Being intentional about incorporating different traditions, and inviting people to experience something new, even if uncomfortable at times, will help your community to thrive in spite of different preferences.

Learn to Love the Chaos

Doug and I once attended a seminar on multi-cultural ministry. The first thing that the speaker said was that if you are part of a multi-cultural community and there isn't any chaos, you are doing it wrong! Hallelujah. We breathed a sigh of relief and hung on every word the presenter had for us after that. We were often frustrated by the lack of smooth functionality we experienced at Immanuel. Why were we having to reinvent our leadership wheel all the time? Why was it so hard to make progress on certain things? Because we were also intentionally seeking to be inclusive, to raise up leaders from various backgrounds and experiences, to move away from a North American model of doing things all the time, to be open to allowing others to lead in their own way, even though it was foreign to us, and at times seemed less efficient. In the end, efficiency isn't always the highest goal. Inclusivity is. I'm not saying that these are mutually exclusive, but to some degree, the more you include others, the less straight-forward your collective path will be. Empowering others means truly freeing them to lead and minister with their own style and gifts. Boundaries and parameters can be set, but there also needs to be room for change and varying perspectives.

Count the Costs, Reap the Rewards

While the benefits are many and the return on one's investment is great, it is important to count the costs of becoming more welcoming so that churches don't venture into this practice only to quit in frustration. Diversity requires listening to one another and allowing the desire for community to supersede the need to be right. Welcoming newcomers means that you can't leave your ministry on autopilot or expect that everyone will just get on board with the way we've always done things. Truly welcoming people means inviting their point of view, giving them a seat at the table, and valuing their perspective and experience; all of which involve sacrificing the status quo. People might leave; change can be uncomfortable and some people prefer a homogenous community. You may not grow as fast as you'd hoped. You will have to repeat your vision over and over. Constantly getting people on board takes extra effort. You will need to find ways to train people to communicate welcome in their words, actions, and attitudes. You may get push-back from resistant members. You yourself will have to change. Do you think your church is willing to count the costs involved in being a more welcoming community? Because if you aren't honest about the things that will be difficult, you will never fully make the changes you need to make in order to be a more welcoming community. Sad as this reality may be, it is far better to own an unwillingness to change than to pretend to be open and not change at all.

7

Welcome Visitors In

CURIOUS ABOUT HOW EXACTLY international churches have helped people to find places of belonging in their new homelands, I held interviews with people from four different international congregations and had many informal conversations with people during the year that we spent at the American Church in Paris. The congregations where I heard stories included the aforementioned Immanuel International Fellowship in Stockholm, the American Church in London, where we served as interim pastors for ten months; the American Church in Paris where we served as interim pastors for ten months; All Nations Church in Luxembourg where we spent four months covering for a pastor on parental leave; and the United Methodist English speaking church of Vienna. Through these compelling and rich conversations, I was able to recognize some recurring themes.

The obvious needs to be stated: that the English language itself is an initial attraction for most visitors living abroad, especially those who, upon arrival, have little or no competency in the local language. It bears mentioning, however, that even those who are or become fluent in the host country's language still tend to have an easier time finding their place in an international church. Language matters. It becomes less important as people integrate and assimilate into their new homelands, and it takes a lot more than a common language for people to feel welcomed in a church, but it's a start. Sometimes it's the culture of openness to difference that matters more than language. Many people native to the host country, for whom language was no barrier at all, also find a more conducive spiritual home in the international church

In my interviews, the following emerged as some of the most consistently compelling reasons people found their church to be a primary place of belonging in their new homeland.

A Pastoral Connection

If I were to rank the reasons people gave for returning to a church, the number one answer would be that they made a personal connection with the pastor. Perhaps this seems unexpected, but when one considers the deep longing for significance that accompanies a move to a new place, maybe it isn't all that surprising. For many, knowing that they are on the pastor's radar helps them feel seen as a person. New arrivals often feel invisible in their new setting. The dominant culture moves along like a fast-moving stream. For those first stepping into a river of cultural "norms" that are anything but, the current feels fast and dangerous. Because the majority culture around them is so used to the movement of the river, they barely notice it, nor do they immediately recognize when someone else may be having a hard time finding their footing.

New people show up at church with all these anxieties occasioned by their new lives, so when they receive a personal touch from the person that is perceived to be the most important person in the congregation, it shores up their sense of self-worth. (I am by no means asserting that the pastor is the most important person in a church, only that he or she often appears to be so to someone new to the community.) Additionally, many people come from cultural backgrounds where the pastor is held in such high regard that only similarly esteemed leaders in the congregation could get close to the pastor. Meeting the pastor conveys a sense of having won respect.

Because the pastor often knows the most people in a church, the pastor is in a unique position to connect people with others from their home country or with similar concerns or interests. In other cases, people felt that if they could connect with the pastor, then surely it would be easy to connect with others. Whether the pastor was or made the introduction, everyone I spoke with recognized that someone already on the inside served as their entry point to the community. I have heard it said that if a visitor doesn't connect with another person at the church within the first three weeks, they won't come back. No matter how compelling the preaching, how wonderful the music, or how good the kids' programs, youth ministry, or social outreach might be, people need other people to acknowledge that they matter before they can envision themselves making a church home.

A Welcoming Presence

A second overwhelmingly popular response was that the place felt welcoming. Explanations for the ethos of a place can be elusive, but let's try to define that abstract a little more concretely. What are the qualities that have mattered to you when sizing up whether or not you are welcome? Does it have to do with decor and the way the room is set up? Are the pews super far away from the pulpit thus creating distance between pastor and congregants? Is there an unspoken dress code that is obvious right away when someone who "didn't get the memo" walks in? Do people keep to themselves, never bothering to look up or look around to see with whom they are worshipping? Are newcomers left to fend for themselves in terms of understanding where to go, getting a program, where to take their kids, or following the liturgy in a clear manner? Are there things in the service that only an insider would know, like when to stand and shake hands, or how long the greeting period goes on, or when and where the kids go for children's time or Sunday School? Sharing information is welcoming. Knowledge is belonging. The more people know about how the church functions, the more at home they feel. A designated space for visitors to get information is key. They need clear directions about where to find the bathrooms, classrooms, and nursery, how the service proceeds, and where to go when it ends.

What about that nursery? If you have a desire for families with small children to join you in worship, it is essential that you provide a space where either their children can be cared for by trusted volunteers or where the parents can care for them themselves while still enjoying the service. Do not underestimate the importance of this ministry. It doesn't have to be a state-of-the-art facility, but it has to be clean, comfortable, and safe. At Immanuel International, we were hemmed in by space issues. The best we could do for a nursery was to provide a room with some toys and chairs. One parent of each child using the room had to stay with their children or arrange with other adults to care for them. We broadcasted the service via short circuit TV and provided songsheets for them so they could follow the songs, as they were not able to see the screens in the sanctuary where the words were projected. It was certainly not ideal, but people expressed time and again what a gift it was to be able to "participate" in the service and at least hear a bit of the sermon. If your church doesn't make any effort at all to provide for parents with children younger than the Sunday School age, your church makes it that much harder for people with babies and toddlers to attend. Parents will conclude that it is not worth the immense effort it takes to get out the door with a little one when they don't get to enjoy the service anyway. This is just one example. Think about your own experiences and consider the key things that helped you to feel welcomed in a new space. Work at implementing these things in your own church.

Mindfulness of the Stranger's Perspective

Long-term members need to develop an awareness of where their church community may have developed blind spots regarding how difficult it might be for a new person to fit in. Let's assume that your church worships on Sunday mornings. When Sundays become automatic, or new people aren't coming so often, or a feeling of comfort with the status quo takes over, you can be sure that the level of welcome for newcomers has decreased. Whether your church is more inclined to formal worship styles or is loose as a goose when it comes to how the service unfolds, there are ways to ensure that the welcome of newcomers remains wide and deep. Overstating the obvious is a good place to start. I return to the metaphor of someone new stepping into a stream that everyone else has been standing in for years. It's important to regularly evaluate the practices common to your worship services that might not be common to others. Honestly assess how easy it would be for someone who has never been to your church before to step into the flow of a typical worship service without feeling lost or bewildered. Don't sing songs that aren't printed somewhere and be sure to tell people where in the hymnal they can find the words. Print what words you are using for the Lord's Prayer and any creedal statement you may recite during your service. Something as simple as the Lord's Prayer can create all kinds of anxiety for people. Do you say sins, trespasses or debts? Over-explain how one takes communion: Do you stand or sit? Dip or drink? Are you using wine or grape juice? Are there a gluten-free or non-alcoholic options available? No one wants to feel insecure about arrangements that have been made for their children. Whether you have a "cry room," a staffed nursery, or Sunday School for kids of all ages, articulate these options, along with instructions on how to recover the children after the service, clearly. Yes, reiterating these things might be slightly tiresome for those at ease in the stream, but it is balm for the nervous newcomer.

Teach and Nurture Openness

A welcoming church resists the temptation to exist mainly for its own membership. A welcoming church is ready to shift a bit in order to accommodate a newcomer. A welcoming church expects long-term members to tolerate a little repetition in the announcements because they understand that for someone, it is new information. Devote some time to honestly assess what aspects of your worship gathering might feel exclusionary to the newcomer. Cultivate an attitude of respect for all visitors who enter your doors. Teach and nurture the perspective that regardless of one's situation, all are welcome here, if that is indeed your belief as a church.

As I already mentioned, you first need to do some work with your congregation to establish if becoming a truly welcoming church is something you really want to do before you can do any meaningful work in living into it. Be honest with yourselves. Don't say you want to be welcoming of all regardless of their situation if you don't mean it. And I mean mean-it-from-the-heart mean it. It's easy to say that all are welcome here, but when the person from another culture or background shows up, someone from a different ethnicity than that of the majority culture, someone with political views that are wildly different than your own, or someone who holds an entirely different world view than the majority of the congregation shows up, are they truly welcome? How is that communicated? How are they embraced and made to feel that you really do want them to stay? It's worth naming the fears that people might feel with being a truly welcoming church. A commitment to a warm and inviting welcome needs to be practiced. It requires a willingness to adopt a non-judgmental point of view toward people regardless of the path that they are on. This can be done by instilling an ever-deepening sense of the truth that all people are created in the image of God and therefore have a core identity as a child of God. It also acknowledges that people can profess faith in the same Christ but hold varying world views, political perspectives, and social values. Different isn't wrong. It's just different. As Christians, we must all do our part to ensure that our view of all humanity is shaped by John 3:16—that God so loves the whole world, including people who have a vastly different background than we do, who look very different from us, whose socio-economic circumstances vary wildly from our own, and whose values and customs may be as foreign to us as ours are to them. Nurturing an attitude of openness requires a commitment and resolve to overcome our own fears and assumptions. We need to allow the motivating force of God's love for the whole of humanity to be central to our lives.

We love to sing that Jesus loves all of the children of the world, but is your church truly committed to welcoming every color, every race as they reflect God's face?

Practical Tips for Creating a More Welcoming Atmosphere

1. *Set up a welcome center and team.* In interviewing people about their experiences as newcomers, I learned that they appreciated a friendly hello, but what they appreciated even more was information about the place they had taken the trouble to come and check out. At Immanuel International we had visitors fill out a newcomer card with basic contact information. These cards were available at a welcome center, positioned directly outside of the sanctuary, where a human being greeted the visitors and assisted them. It's important to remember that newcomers are nervous when they arrive. Having someone greeting them and showing them where to go goes a long way in reducing that anxiety. Remember too, that when the service ends, visitors often don't know what to do or where to go. Describe and invite them to stay for whatever fellowship practice your church employs. Having a designated space where a visitor can go and find someone to talk to often puts them at ease. Urge your longer-term members to use part of the post-church time to stop and introduce themselves to people who appear to be newcomers. People sometimes hesitate to do this because they feel embarrassed if it turns out the person isn't new. Encourage a lighthearted response; it's as easy as saying something like "well, you're new to me." Set up a roster of folks whose primary job it is on a Sunday is to walk around and look for new people to welcome.

   My interviewees said that when volunteers actually walked with them to their kids' Sunday School classes and spelled out clearly for them what the procedures were, it was very helpful. In the case of foreign visitors, many said that once a church member or the pastor learned where they were from, they sought to connect them to people from the same country or background. If there is a specific Bible study or home group that seems well-suited to their age or where they live, connect the newcomer with the leader. Make sure that your welcome hosts have up-to-date information about what is happening in the life of the church so that they can pass that along to the newcomer. Have clear directives about how to access a church calendar, a website or a newsletter.

A solid system for following up with visitors should also be in place. In the week after coming to Immanuel International, visitors received a welcome email from one of the pastors. Every six weeks we held a newcomer gathering in our home after the service and invited long-time members, often members of the council, to join us in welcoming these newcomers. Again, many were moved by getting an invitation to the pastors' home so soon after their arrival. They appreciated the personal touch in being invited to learn more. This helped them feel seen and cared for, which is what newcomers are primarily searching for. Of course, the larger the church, the more difficult these personal contacts from the pastor become, but I'm convinced that anyone who reaches out to make a personal connection on behalf of the church will be well-received and will make a difference in the life of the newcomer. One thing that I have noticed about the US is that there is often no fellowship gathering after the service. This makes it harder to connect with new people, which makes having a welcome center all the more important. Not every visitor will stop by, but those wanting a deeper connection most certainly will. A staffed welcome center and a clear plan for following through with visitors goes a long way in ensuring that interested visitors will connect with at least one interested human being during their visit to your church.

2. *Present the opportunity to serve early and often.* We often make the mistake in the church of waiting too long before asking newcomers to lend a hand. Because the nature of the international church involves constant change, we learned

early on to get people plugged into ministry right away. Whether they were going to be in Stockholm for a short time or were planning on immigrating and making it their new home, it was always time for them to take the next step to involvement. The opportunity to serve and contribute to a community is central to thinking of it as our own; don't deny it to people because you're afraid of scaring them off. In any church, there are countless tasks that almost anyone can do with minimal training: ushering, serving coffee, helping with sound and tech. Skilled musicians, liturgists, youth workers, and Sunday School teachers need to be sought out, asked to join the ministry, and trained. Leaving these gifts unused in the church is a cardinal sin! Of course, the action of assessing gifts requires some time spent getting to know people in order to best determine where they might be able to serve, a process that can also create meaningful bonds. Guiding people in discovering and using their gifts should be part of the subculture of your church. The overall culture should be one of involvement, not of sitting on the sidelines. Making room for new members to truly contribute might entail some longer-term members stepping back and deferring to fresh ideas. Fewer things frustrate me more than being asked to serve somewhere, agreeing to do so, then realizing that I'm merely a warm body rather than a voice people genuinely want to listen to.

During our time at Immanuel International, Doug and I saw how different cultures respond to the need for volunteers differently. In some cultures, the needs are readily observed, and people raise their hand to meet them. In other cultures, people see the needs, but feel that volunteering to address them would be overstepping if no one asks them to. In still other cultures, needs may not be easy for the uninitiated to spot. Consequently, we learned that we needed to recruit volunteers in a variety of ways. When we were preparing to leave Immanuel International, I came to learn that the "word on the street" was that if Pastor Jodi came to talk to you,

you knew you were going to be volunteering because it was impossible for people to say no to me. Wow, if only I had known my superpower from the beginning! But I did realize that when taking the time to sit down with someone and talk through their gifts and discern with them where they could be an asset to the ministry, the willingness to serve was much higher. Yes, it takes time. It's harder than getting them to fill out a form, but it's often what it takes to open the door for people from different backgrounds to say yes to serving in the church.

3. *Encourage people to connect with others from their home country or with an affinity group.* This might be surprising advice for anyone who has never lived as a foreigner. Foreigners are often criticized for wanting to be separate from the host country, seeking to remain in their own culture rather than assimilating to their new homeland. I will speak more about the differences between integration and assimilation a bit later, but for now let me say that both integrating with the new culture and maintaining your roots are important. Remember that when a person new to the culture or community shows up to your church on a Sunday, he or she has already had an exhausting week in a foreign environment: struggling with the language, confused by the culture, tired of feeling like an outsider all the time. We learned to acknowledge that people needed time to be with others from their home country along with needing opportunities to meet and interact with others outside of their cultural groups.

It's okay for people to want to cleave to their own culture. There are language issues, cultural differences, and even unique ways to catch up on the news from home. Let's face it, as an American, it wasn't very fruitful for me to discuss Major League Baseball with friends from Uganda! But when I had the chance to get with other Americans, it was fun to have a foundation of local knowledge from my home country that could go unspoken and be built upon. It also affirms that one's native identity which, while perhaps shifting, isn't disappearing. Remember, we all desire to be seen. Constantly tamping down the parts of oneself that others wouldn't understand makes a person feel even more invisible. Being with others from one's own homeland provides opportunity to experience that old familiarity and understanding. Allowing for opportunities for like-minded folks to interact without pressure to further integrate is essential. Keep in mind that affinity groups can be focused on direct discipleship, like a Bible study or lecture series, or on demographic-specific gatherings, but they can all catalyze building relationships. Sports groups, choirs, hiking clubs, service ministries, and book clubs all help people to connect with others and deepen their sense of belonging.

4. *Set up partnerships between newcomers and long-time members.* Matching longer term members with newcomers is a great way to help people build relationships with those who are different than they are, while reducing the sources of anxiety the newcomer has to navigate in a new homeland. Providing partnerships to negotiate issues of banking, finding a doctor, grocery shopping, finding the best bargains, and signing kids up for sports and other after-school activities, goes a long way in helping a newcomer get settled. Meanwhile, for those who know the ropes, getting to know a foreigner in this intentional manner will also illuminate their perspective on how complex life is for someone new to their society. Both parties can learn so much from one another, and the emergence of these cross-cultural relationships will provide energy and joy to your community.

5. *Invite foreigners to share in your holiday traditions.* Let's face it, adjusting to the holiday traditions in a new country can be exciting at first but can also lead to feelings of deep alienation. Including a foreigner in your family's traditions is one of the most powerful ways we can say to someone that we truly want them here. It does indeed require a sacrifice on your part to open the door of your home to a stranger on these sacred occasions, but that is part of what it means to reflect the wide embrace of Christ in your daily life. Be aware

of how the holiday rhythms of a society impact newcomers. For instance, in Sweden, most Swedes take the entire month of July off. Many Swedes have a summer place where they can retreat from the demands of the rest of the year and lounge in the long hours of daylight that the Nordic summer brings. For many internationals, there is no summer home and often, a lack of financial resources for a long holiday escape. This is another time that foreigners can feel out of step with the local culture. Many from our international fellowship could only manage "staycations," that is, vacation from work while staying put at home. Being out of step with a culture that values this month-long holiday can feel very isolating for those not participating. With their neighbors gone and shops and programs shut down for the month, familiar feelings of loneliness and isolation can creep back in. Recognizing this dynamic, we developed a summer program that helped to gather our community in meaningful ways while the rest of the nation headed to their summer places. To our surprise and delight, we had some of our most fruitful and fun ministry times together while the Swedes were on vacation.

Doug and I hosted an open house on Christmas for anyone needing a place to gather. Many foreigners adopted the Swedish custom of opening of gifts at family gatherings on Christmas Eve, but this meant that feelings of homesickness and missing family could be felt most acutely on Christmas Day. In fact, the first year that we had the open house, we did so to combat my own Christmas Day blues! That first year we had about twenty people join us in our home. Through the years, as our open house became part of people's traditions, we would have about a hundred folks come through. The advantage for us as pastors in doing this was that whenever we met people who didn't have anywhere to go on Christmas, we were able to simply offer an open invitation to our home, which could accommodate a large number of people. This isn't something that everyone can do nor would it work on Christmas in other places. The point to ponder for your community is what similar need might the strangers in your midst have and how might your local members staunch their loneliness around the holidays a bit?

Large formal gatherings are by no means the only way to foster a culture of hospitality at your church. Encourage more established people to bring someone new home no matter the time of year. The power of an invitation to come to someone's home is hard to estimate. And think of the joy you can bring someone as they enter your traditions and experience something new for the first time!

6. *Create less traditionally churchy ways for people to enter your community and get connected.* Fellowship events that allow for the emergence of casual relationships to be nurtured are key. If you offer such events often enough, you will always have somewhere fun to invite newcomers. Children's programs, youth events, and fellowship events that are set up for the express purpose of connecting people are important ways for people to be able to get to know one another in nonthreatening ways. Studying scripture, worshiping together, and spending time in prayer are wonderful ways to deepen friendships and bolster one's spiritual journey, but providing the opportunity to laugh together, have fun, and relax in each other's company is equally important for abiding friendships.

8

Distinguish Between Integration and Assimilation

ONE OF THE MORE challenging aspects of bringing together a multi-cultural community is ensuring a true blending of cultures as opposed to one dominant culture setting the tone for all others. For a long time, diverse communities were touted as melting pots where all cultures came together and merged into one new flavor. But sharp critiques have been made, claiming that those on the bottom usually get burned while the scum rises to the top. Miguel De La Torre observes,

> In effect, those with power and privilege are able to impose a system that protects their lifestyle from the criticism of those living on the margins of society. Therefore liberation from oppression can only occur when those struggling for a voice cease trying to assimilate into something that they are not. Probably the greatest lie of the melting pot paradigm is that if we simply assimilate, we will be accepted. Like a salad, we are all distinct. For the salad is not one element, but many. Unlike the melting pot paradigm, a truer American cultural salad retains the differing flavors of its diverse roots while enriching all other elements. The lettuce cannot say to the tomato, "Why aren't you lettuce? Nor can the broccoli tell the

pickle, 'You must assimilate and become like broccoli". Each separate element is distinctively celebrated, while together becoming something greater than the sum of its parts.¹

Admittedly, the salad metaphor only plays out so far, but it hints at something more akin to integration than assimilation. In any gathering of people, there will tend to be a dominant group that holds much of the power. The very nature of adopting a multicultural profile means that profound shifts are bound to occur, simply because each group that joins brings its own understanding of the unspoken rules by which a community should function. This is where some of the most profound conflict can emerge with communities that are seeking to be more diverse in nature. Understanding the differences between the integration conversation and the assimilation conversation is key to navigating some of that conflict. Notice how I didn't say avoiding the conflict. Conflict will inevitably occur. It's how we navigate it that determines the relative success of our efforts.

Sadiq Khan, the mayor of London, England, who is from an immigrant family, answered this way when asked about the difference between integration and assimilation.

> Assimilation is generally defined as adopting the ways of another culture and fully becoming part of a different society. Whereas integration is typically defined as incorporating individuals from different groups into a society as equals. The difference is subtle but significant.²

The difference is indeed subtle but significant. Assimilation is a term the dominant group often avoids using because it has unpleasantly xenophobic connotations. It smacks of pushing foreigners to ditch their own cultural identities to become indistinguishable from the host culture. Change is hard, so if you are part of the majority

1. De La Torre, "The problem with the melting pot.", https://www.ethicsdaily.com/the-problem-with-the-melting-pot-cms-13647/

2. O'Brien, "The important difference between assimilation and integration."https://www.immigrationreform.com/2016/09/29/the-important-difference-between-assimilation-and-integration/

holding much of the power and often much of the money, why do it? Assimilation demands less of the dominant group in the way of change, thus allowing its members to maintain a certain comfort level by shunting the bulk of the discomfort of adapting onto others; in their mind, the minority parties shoulder all of the responsibility for changing. The inherent injustice of this system aside, it doesn't work. If the dominant culture's value system doesn't accommodate those of the other cultures you won't have a unified community with shared values, but a divided society scrapping over resources. The majority group's subtle or blatant pressure on the minority communities causes frustration and conflict at all levels when things don't go as desired. Sadly then, the minority culture is often labeled difficult or disinterested in integration and thus blamed for a structure that wasn't fair to them from the start.

Perhaps some stories from our years at Immanuel can help to illuminate this. Immanuel Church is a Swedish church with a wonderful facility and strong financial resources. Three churches sold their properties in the early 1970s and joined together to form one church, purchasing property in a very desirable location in central Stockholm. They also formed a real estate company and began to purchase properties all over Stockholm, building a high-quality hotel on the same block that the new church stood on. The economic brilliance behind this move is indisputable. The capital from the real estate ventures helps to fund the church's ministry and building; many wonderful things have resulted from the economic freedom supported by this model. The early vision of Immanuel Church to welcome immigrants and refugees into their midst is also beautiful. Seeing a large influx of Korean immigrants, the church founded a Korean fellowship and called and hired a pastor from South Korea to come and lead this group. A few years later, many refugees from various African nations were coming into Sweden. Recognizing the need for an English language Bible study/worship experience for them, the church founded an international fellowship. A pastor from a sister denomination in the US was asked to come and lead this group. The vision and mission of the Swedish congregation to provide worship experiences for these immigrants in their own language was impressive and enthusiastically supported. Over the years, both groups grew. The mantra from the Swedish fellowship was that Immanuel is one church with three equal fellowships, however, the equality of the fellowships was often disputed by the non-Swedish populations.

Money Matters

As in many churches, matters pertaining to money and how it was allocated were a source of tension. The budget process highlights one of the ways that the Swedish fellowship had dominance over the minority fellowships. In the early stages, Immanuel Church established budgets for the English language group, called the International Fellowship, and the Korean language group, called the Korean Fellowship. Funding for all of the fellowships largely came from the Swedish church (and its lucrative real estate holdings) as the fledgling fellowships were unable to support themselves. Because the minority groups started as ministries of the Swedish fellowship, each group held one simple line in a very complex budget that included whole categories for things like music, youth, mission, deacon work, outreach, general administration, personnel, retreats, and so on. The implication became that the other budgeted items were for the Swedish ministry only. Music for the international and Korean fellowships was not included in the overall music budget. The youth budget was only for the Swedish group, and so on. This proved to be an unfair comparison for the International and Korean fellowships and created a great deal of tension between the fellowship groups. This is a classic example of how the dominant group, the Swedish fellowship in this case, gave themselves a budgetary advantage. The minority groups remained line items in a large Swedish budget rather than having the chance to budget for their own needs regarding music, youth, etc.

You can only imagine the ill will this practice often created. It made the minority congregations feel assimilated into the Swedish budget instead of being integrated to the overall financial picture of Immanuel church. Whenever cuts were necessary and the allocation of resources became competitive, the international and Korean fellowships often felt that they were not given a fair chance since their overall budgets were being compared with mere line items in the Swedish budget. As the international fellowship grew, staff was added and the ministry needs increased. Subsequently, the giving also increased. But by maintaining the international fellowship's position as a line item of the overall church, it became increasingly frustrating to justify the budgetary increases because of consistently being compared to the line item budgets of the Swedish ministry. This practice subtly kept the international and Korean fellowships in a subordinate category to the Swedish fellowship, rather than allowing them to emerge as equal partners. At times, one could sense the tension it created among the Swedish members as well, communicating as it did that the internationals and Koreans were "taking" money from the Swedish group, even though both the Korean and international fellowships had, at times, stronger giving practices than the Swedish group.

Worship Life

Beyond money matters, one of the most profound ways that the Swedish ministry often put such pressure on the international and Korean fellowships to conform to their way of doing things manifested when the three groups celebrated worship together. Our usual practice was to have the three different groups worshipping at the same time in their own space, language and style. Immanuel church was incredibly blessed to have enough space in their building to be able to have three different worship services going on at the same time without interfering with one another! As an act of solidarity and unity, we occasionally celebrated joint worship services. This is a great and necessary aspect of existing together as one church with three language groups, but the actual planning and implementation of the worship services was often quite difficult.

For starters, the planning meetings were often comprised of a single pastor each from the international fellowship and the

Korean fellowship, along with two or three pastors from the Swedish fellowship and two or three musicians or other worship participants from the Swedish fellowship. It is easy to see how imbalanced this approach was from the beginning. Additionally, because of the sanctuary size and the installed organ, the Swedish sanctuary was always the default sanctuary for these joint worship services. The international and Korean groups were thus always asked to make the biggest physical change when these services were held. There was definitely some appeal in meeting in the larger sanctuary and getting to use the organ, but it lacked the intimacy of the smaller sanctuaries.

Dealing in three languages, we were forced to keep the services fairly simple. The large sanctuary also had headphones for simultaneous translation, which was wonderful for those who needed that. The Swedish lead pastor and musicians often used the standard Swedish service as a template, making for a worship style that differed greatly from that of the international and Korean fellowships. So not only were we asking our people to come to a service in a different room, while dealing with languages that many didn't understand, we were also asking them to adopt an entirely new way of worship that was dramatically different than what the International fellowship was accustomed to week in, week out. Often these changes proved to be too much and sadly, more than one-third of our regular attenders just decided not to come. They felt it was too much work. While this was understandable, we urged people to overcome their discomfort a few times a year because we saw the value in the three fellowships finding ways to come together as one church through worship.

But only to a point. We also felt that no more than three or four joint services a year were appropriate because of how much extra planning time it required, how much shifting it required of the international fellowship, and because so many members chose to not come. The joint services did not help us minister to the international community or welcome new visitors effectively. In contrast, the Swedish fellowship often enjoyed the joint services more because it drew more people into their worship space and enhanced their existing worship service. It was difficult for the Swedish leadership to understand why the International fellowship didn't enjoy the joint service as much as the Swedish group did. We tried to explain that if the services were held in our sanctuary with the dominant style being that of the international fellowship, then perhaps some of their congregants might not enjoy the combined services as much either. It became increasingly frustrating to feel pressured to fit into the Swedish model when the services themselves really should have been a true reflection of the three different groups. Over time this did improve, but that's in part because Doug and I resisted a lot of the pressure to assimilate into the Swedish way of doing church and in the process gained a reputation for being difficult to work with and not wanting to integrate. We were willing to negotiate but wanted to be met by an equal willingness on the part of the Swedish group. Had we been able to consistently execute a fully integrated joint service, the following things would be important.

1. The order of service would be freshly crafted, fully integrating aspects of each fellowship's worship services, with all parties compromising.
2. The music would reflect each tradition and not be dominated by a certain style, even if one group strongly disliked the style of another fellowship.
3. The worship participants would reflect broadly all fellowships, with each seeking lay people to participate in the service.

As the years went by, the planning process shifted to include the above-mentioned values in a more consistent manner. The most successful aspect of our joint services was around the communion table where language didn't matter and our traditions all dove-tailed nicely. Perhaps around the table of our Lord is where a diverse, fully-integrated community should find equal footing. In spite of the difficulties, we did share in some wonderful joint worship experiences together and many valued these times of crossover with one another.

Post-Service Fellowship Time

One might think that getting together after the service for a cup of coffee and a cinnamon roll would not create any conflict at all. What's not to love about the Swedish tradition known as *fika*, i.e. coffee and a little something to eat? People valued this fellowship time so much that when the international fellowship grew to two services, people said they'd only get on board if we offered a fellowship *fika* after both services! All of the language groups had a coffee or tea time after their weekly worship services but all three planned, implemented, and paid for their fellowship time in very different ways.

The Swedish group charged a fee for coffee and treats, and it was expected that all who partook paid. The Korean group made their own treats, so participants just took turns providing the treats for that group and no payment was expected. The international fellowship built the expense for coffee fellowship into their budget and asked for donations from those who could and wanted to chip in a bit. Three equally reasonable yet very different ways of accomplishing the same thing, yet remarkably, one of the aspects of the joint services that created the most conflict. The Swedes were angry with the internationals because they assumed they wanted their treats for free. And the internationals were frustrated because it was just one more thing that was different for them than the usual protocol for Sundays. A deeper concern for us as the pastors was the reality that for many families in the international fellowship, the cost of buying the treat for their whole family was too expensive. The international fellowship had more low-income participants than the Swedish group because many were foreigners or immigrants who were unable to secure higher paying jobs in Swedish society. We never wanted anyone to feel they couldn't participate in the fellowship time because they couldn't afford it.

The way each group paid for the coffee fellowship illuminates a more complex issue related to the budget. The international fellowship preferred to adopt the policy of building budgetary support for the various aspects of our ministry that were going to cost money and operate on a donation basis, knowing that we'd have to supplement the expenses from our budget. This worked well for us. The giving of our participants supported this system. Some from the Swedish group interpreted the international fellowship not paying directly for our after-service activities as stealing from or taking advantage of the system. Some ugly remarks were made that tainted the environment during these coffee times. Our inability to work out a genuinely clear system for the days that we had joint services led to a lot of conflict and misunderstanding between people whom the joint services were intended to bring together. Sadly, many people from the international fellowship came away feeling unwelcome and many Swedes walked away with a very negative view of their international brothers and sisters.

Our inability to work through these issues on an upper management level was due in part to our different cultural values. We repeatedly asked that the charge for the coffee be waived at joint services and instead, solicit donations. All of the groups could budget a bit more for the fellowship time on joint service days so that no one felt cheated. But even here it was hard for the Swedish group to agree to this because they felt so strongly about ensuring that everyone paid for their coffee. The explanation that we do pay, we just do it through a central budget rather than out of individual's pockets, seemed to fall on deaf ears. It didn't take long to figure out that societal attitudes towards immigrants and people of color were manifesting inside the church.

Even when the giving of the International fellowship began to surpass that of the Swedish group, cultural bias continued to spin the false narrative among many of the Swedes that the members of the international fellowship, often people of color, were unwilling to pay for things. Our coffee hour, intended to help us overcome our prejudices had become another arena for them to play out.

Combined Sunday School

One would think that with all of the groups worshiping at the same time, combined Sunday School classes would be a relatively easy logistic to pull off. In the international and Korean fellowship groups we always had children who spoke Swedish but not English or Korean, so offering Sunday School in a language these kids could understand was challenging. At some point we began to talk about an integrated Sunday School class, in Swedish, that children from all fellowship groups could attend. The kids would all start in their respective worship services and at a designated time, gather in the room where the combined class would take place. The Swedish fellowship would take charge of this. After a few weeks, it became clear that it wasn't going to work, and the Swedish group called it quits. The reasons for it not working out were complex but worth examining.

To begin with, there was a cultural disconnect in that the international fellowship offered Sunday School every Sunday of the year whereas the Swedish group took Sundays off during school holidays or other events that mattered to them but not to the international congregants. Additionally, the Swedish group was a bit overwhelmed by the number of children from the international group. Instead of rejoicing and adjusting, they decide it was impossible to deal with such a large group of children. On top of that, some of the children from the international fellowship were more mischievous than others and didn't behave in "proper Swedish fashion" and were therefore deemed unruly and out of line. Granted, one of the difficulties in staffing this joint Sunday School class was the reality that the parents of the international children didn't speak adequate Swedish to feel competent to lead classes. Thus, the pressure to staff this class rested firmly on the shoulders of the Swedes. Another sad reality we heard referenced was that the Swedish children were sometimes intimidated by children of color.

When the Swedes were no longer willing to engage these issues, the failure of this attempt at integration was deeply hurtful to the smaller groups. No one from the Swedish side accused their own community members who oversaw the Sunday School of being unwilling to integrate. It was simply accepted as something that was never going to work very well. This is something that the dominant group must watch out for: giving themselves a pass when they don't have the energy and/or ability to meet the challenge of integration, while being highly critical of other groups when they resist something or want to execute it in a different manner.

Combined Confirmation

Another example of learning to walk the fine line between assimilation and integration occurred while seeking to provide a confirmation experience for the youth of the international and Swedish fellowships. Confirmation is a major rite of passage for Swedish young people. Most Swedish fourteen-year-olds will go through Confirmation even if neither they nor their family regularly practice any faith tradition. In some cases, Swedish youth who have not been in a church since their infant baptism sign up for Confirmation. The opposite could be said for most of the youth in the international fellowship. Raised in Christian homes and attending Sunday School from the age they were eligible, most of our young people were active in the youth group and were exploring and cultivating their own faith. So while both groups were offering Confirmation, the curricular goals and depth of conversation about matters of faith that could be held were vastly different. How were we to offer an integrated experience for these kids while accomplishing the very different goals the programs had? No easy answers here!

Additionally, we had some theological differences to iron out. The Swedish group had longstanding traditions and curriculum that did not suit the international fellowship's goals for Confirmation. We felt that the cultural and theological differences between the two groups could not be ignored. This led to a great deal of tension and frustration with one another.

In spite of the challenges, an attempt was made to have the groups meet together and our youth pastor was an active participant. For the most part, the youth enjoyed each other's company and forged some warm friendships. The fact that the international youth had a more advanced faith and knowledge of the Bible than the Swedish youth caused some awkwardness. Four other significant difficulties arose. First, the subject of cost again became an issue. Swedish Confirmation included a longer camp experience and was quite expensive for some of our families. This created some tension around who could afford confirmation and who could not. Secondly, for the Swedish group, the confirmation experience was often more of an outreach ministry, while for the Internationals it was more about discipleship. Both important and valuable, but this certainly created challenges around how to pull off both at the same time within the same program. Thirdly, the students from the Swedish group largely ceased attending Immanuel once the program ended; the international students felt the sudden loss of their friendship keenly when the course ended. Fourthly, we were seeing an increase in students coming to the international fellowship who did not speak fluent or even basic Swedish, and the language barrier was becoming more apparent.

These obvious differences caused Doug and me to re-think the joint program. When we made known our concerns and expressed our desire to run a separate Confirmation experience, some from the Swedish group grew angry and again accused us of not wanting to integrate. Our hurt and frustration was real and we tried to explain the concerns outlined above. It was not so much that we were closed to integrating Confirmation as much as it just seemed like there were too many differences to be able to offer Confirmation in a meaningful manner for all involved. Assimilation didn't suit the overall ministry goals for our youth, so we could not move in that direction; neither would our model serve the Swedish community well. The best solution was to offer a parallel Confirmation for our young people, in English, and led by the youth pastor and the lead pastors of the international fellowship. It gave us an excellent opportunity to connect with the youth during this special season of their lives and it allowed both groups to develop a curriculum that would suit their clientele much better than trying to find something that might work for both groups.

Interestingly enough, the critiques came from the Swedes, not the Internationals. Many from the Swedish fellowship failed to accept the rationale for a separate program, and dismissed as unwilling to integrate. Ultimately, the success of the separate programs was largely overlooked by our critics because of the insistence by some that the only successful outcome was to do joint Confirmation. This insistence came in spite of the facts that the groups ran on different calendars, had different goals, and held our Confirmation Sundays at different times of year.

We learned from these experiences that sometimes when working with diverse communities, integrating is not the best option. There are times when allowing language and cultural differences to stand is appropriate and should not be seen as a failure to incorporate diversity. The danger emerges when one group is angry about this because they want the minority culture to assimilate. We often attempted integrated programs with both groups that didn't succeed as well as the more demographically tailored programs. While we did find ways to gather the groups together occasionally and friendships were formed across the cultural differences, we regret that this did not work out more often. Sometimes the combined energy of all parties just is not enough to overcome the challenge.

This is something the majority group must always check themselves on. If they don't have the energy for a truly integrated experience, they must always be careful that they don't default to pressuring the other groups to assimilate while calling it integration. Assimilation requires very little change from the majority group while demanding the minority groups conform to majority rule. Ideally both groups will find the energy to make changes that allow them to draw closer to understanding their differences and creating new traditions and experiences that honor both groups' expectations and desires.

A wise leader and trusted friend of mine was asked, "What do you think other church communities could/should learn from Immanuel as regards welcoming the stranger/foreigner/outsider?" He answered, "Build only on what is theologically uniting and central to faith; hold lightly to denominational traditions; create a plurality of wholesome, eclectic, nourishing, worship ingredients that integrate tradition(s) with innovation while enabling everyone to feel at home and to learn through the experiences of others; resist at all costs the temptation to become a subculture."[3] The degree to which we were able to adhere to these principles determined how successful we were in creating a positive atmosphere for meaningful integration. I outline some areas that didn't function well because sometimes we learn more from our mistakes than our successes. It deserves to be stated that many things did function wonderfully. I commend Immanuel for the vision they continue to have to offer worship in three different languages to vastly diverse populations living in Stockholm. While at times frustrating to try to figure out how to best work at being one church with three congregations, Immanuel remains a great model for how churches can open their doors to diverse populations and be a welcoming place for strangers and immigrants to become friends and members of God's family under one roof.

---

3. Private correspondence, June 24, 2017

9

Practice Meaningful Integration

Now that we've examined some cautionary tales, let's get back to talking about more desirable models of life together. A desire for meaningful relationships that celebrates rather than dilutes the diversity that comprises a community allows people to work hard at meaningful integrating in spite of the challenges that emerge. Even when there are language barriers, finding ways to worship and experience fellowship together are important. If your church is seeking to be more open to the stranger among you, giving some attention to the following issues will be helpful in integrating rather than assimilating these newcomers.

Combined Worship Services

In spite of, and at times maybe even because of, the programming difficulties behind the scenes, our joint services at Immanuel Church were often lovely realizations of the potential of a truly inclusive worship experience. If you are seeking to plan worship integrating two or more culturally distinct communities, or even if you just want to your congregation to intentionally honor and benefit from a few distinct voices in your midst, here are some things to consider in your planning.

Timing and style of worship

Does the joint service always only coincide with the majority culture's time of worship? Ensure that all service times are considered so that the minority culture doesn't always have to be the community who changes its practice. Are the worship styles of the two (or more) communities vastly different? If so, the leaders must work hard at creating an integrated worship service if they want people to experience an authentically shared experience. This will likely mean that members from both communities might experience some discomfort in the service, but this shouldn't be avoided at the expense of reflecting the diversity of people present at the service. The leadership needs to nurture people into valuing something other than comfort when seeking to do this. Encourage people to be open to something new as a means of understanding their brothers and sisters who worship alongside of them. Embedded within this are orders of worship.

None of the communities should insist that certain things be done a certain way, especially when the other community doesn't share the same perspective. In our case, we took the offering before the sermon, while the Koreans only took it after the sermon. Both parties needed to be willing to compromise on this on any given day for the good of the order of worship. It is self-defeating if any group says, "It has to be done like this." Additionally, great care should be taken that any aspect of the service that is totally foreign to the other group(s) be avoided. At Immanuel, the Swedish group had a special liturgy that they shared when someone in the congregation died. They were unwilling to let this go when someone died the week of the joint service. What this meant was that they either had to explain at great length, in Korean and English, what they were doing or just move ahead with it and leave the Internationals and Koreans at a loss for what was happening. Learning to let go of our "sacred cows" when joining together for a more integrated experience is part of what it means to allow for meaningful integration and not forced assimilation.

Translation

Be prepared to offer translation of the key elements of the service but also embrace not fully translating everything, knowing that the Lord understands even if we don't. Of course, when it comes to the sermon, translation should always be provided but certain prayers could be offered in various languages with a summary in the bulletin, people can offer the Lord's prayer in whatever language they choose, songs could be sung in the various languages with textual translation provided, scripture readings could be read in various languages with the references made available for people to follow along in a Bible in their own language. It's wonderful to hear the different languages that God has put on this earth, giving people a deeper appreciation for the global community of Christianity rather than remaining stuck with an impression that their own culture and language are the only language of Christendom.

Always celebrate the Eucharist.

There is no better place to symbolize our unity in Christ than around the table of our Lord. Many wonderful things get accomplished when celebrating communion together. The liturgy does not have to be translated since most people understand what is being celebrated without words. The visual acts around the communion table are wonderfully universal. When selecting servers, choose people from all communities to serve together and to offer the bread and the cup in their own language. This seems elementary, but hearing the words of Christ in another tongue can be quite poignant and affirming of the worldwide communion of saints. For the most part, no matter what other theological differences each community may have, the table fellowship is one place there is little conflict. Celebrate this!

How often?

As previously mentioned, I think Immanuel made the mistake of wanting to do the joint service too often and therefore it became more of a chore than a joy. Three times a year is probably a good target and can be scheduled strategically in order to not create extra burdens for the planning staff during the busiest seasons of the church year. Planning for these services requires a great deal of lead time and effort so be careful to not add to the regular workload of those planning to an extent that their week in, week out responsibilities related to ministry planning get compromised. Also, you have to be careful about how often you push the congregation to do something new and potentially a bit uncomfortable. You don't want to get to a point where more people skip the service than come because that ultimately defeats your purpose. Three times a year provides a regular rhythm but doesn't over-stress the congregation or the leaders.

Invite newcomers into the planning process.

This is central to meaningful integration and the goal of increasing the impact of the newer populations so that they don't feel as though the majority culture is trying to swallow them whole. Far too often people from the majority culture sit down and put their heads together and brainstorm ideas about how to help outsiders feel welcome and wanted in their midst when all would be better served if we empowered the newcomers to share their own ideas. We need to actually value them, their opinions and their experience by putting ourselves in a position to learn from them. No amount of effort put into helping people feel included will accomplish what true inclusion can. Of course, this is hard because the newcomers might bring ideas that require change and discomfort for the established community. But for a truly integrated experience, all sides must move a bit.

A special word regarding the manner in which communities lift up various traditions in their worship life together: While it is fine to have a Sunday dedicated to youth, or the African fellowship or the Filipino group, a good goal is to seek to integrate aspects of these groups into your regular worship life. Learning a few songs from other traditions and incorporating them into your life together is a more integrated and honoring experience for all than simply giving these groups one Sunday where they can "show off" who they are in worship. That divides the congregation into performers and observers rather than inviting us all into full participation. Ensure that people from the tradition being introduced are involved in leading out when introducing these new experiences. The more you coherently and consistently integrate practices from various groups into your worship service, the more inclusive and diverse your services will be over the long haul.

Share the Leadership

While related to the above statement, this takes that principle a step further and pushes the majority group to make room for the minority culture to have a significant role not only in planning, but in contributing to the vision and priorities of the community. Share the pulpit and the worship leading, invite diverse music choices and style, empower the newcomer to welcome the newcomer. Allow people to accomplish their responsibilities in their own style, as long as it suits the overall ethos of what you as a church are trying to achieve.

I know that early on at Immanuel International raising up leaders from certain ethnic groups was a big challenge. For reasons initially unknown, getting people from the African nations and the Filipino communities—who comprised a significant portion of the congregation—to serve on the church board in and in other leadership positions was almost impossible. In Paris, this obvious imbalance was also seen in the make-up of the church council; ethnic groups from countries outside of the European Union and the United States were disproportionately underrepresented in the leadership structure of the church as a whole. When speaking with a member of the nominating committee about this, she said that they do try to recruit leaders from other countries, but they are often unwilling to say yes. Rather than leaving it at that, if a church truly desires to change and become more welcoming and inclusive, work must be done to excavate the reasons behind this reluctance on the part of minority cultures to serve in positions of leadership. Perhaps it has to do with the time that the meetings are held. Or maybe some education is required so they don't feel intimated by the prospect of serving in a capacity where they feel under-equipped and fear doing a poor job or not being able to fulfill the calling. Maybe they come from traditions where lay people were not empowered for leadership. A first-time leader can feel a great deal of pressure to represent their entire ethnic community, especially if they are the sole person from their community on a board or committee. Maybe that's too overwhelming to face.

As Immanuel initially sought to include representatives from the international and Korean fellowships on the predominantly Swedish boards and committees, they did so by asking one person from each of the non-Swedish fellowships to serve on committees with multiple representatives from the Swedish fellowship. While the Swedish leadership had confidence that the other groups were well-represented by this one person, challenges arose because the representatives from the Korean and international communities felt that their single voice was drowned out by the chorus of Swedish voices around the table. This left the leaders from the non-Swedish groups with the impression that their opinions didn't really matter, and often led to no one from the minority groups wanting to serve. Thankfully, over time, Immanuel found a way to achieve more balanced representation on their boards and committees.

Communities would be wise to avoid burdening any one person with representing an entire ethnic or cultural group, or worse, serving only as a token of that group's involvement. The goal is to pursue and achieve diverse, well-represented leadership teams, but in the end, I'm the last person you should be listening to about how to do this. Clearly, those coming from the minority populations and cultures that you are seeking to integrate will have much more insight than I can offer here. Talk to them. Do the work of learning why leaders of color or under-represented groups are not eager to serve in higher levels of leadership, then seek to remove the impediments.

Diversify Your Staff

One of the regrets that I have from our years at Immanuel is that we failed to diversify our staff in any significant manner. We were three white pastors from the United States, and our children's ministry director and our secretary were also white women from the United States. I suppose it helped a bit that I was female, but the fact that we were an all-white staff leading a multi-cultural church was not ideal. The position of worship director was the one position in which we managed some diversity. Through the years, we had Swedes, a black South African, an African American, and a white British couple in that position. I do think that for a church to become truly multi-cultural and more deeply reflect the diversity that it proclaims to value, the staff needs to change to reflect that over time.

If staff turnover is slow, that means fewer opportunities to diversify the staff, and change will be even slower in coming. Maybe part of being deeply committed to diversity entails that staff move on more regularly, making room for others to have a chance. While I loved that we were pastors at Immanuel International for almost seventeen years and enjoyed stability on our staff, I regret that we made so few new hires that we did not have the opportunity to diversify our staff.

Thankfully, we eventually made progress in lifting up lay leaders from all of the represented continents in our fellowship. We ensured that our board was always diverse, including electing chairpersons from countries other than the US and the United Kingdom. We stayed committed to having people who led our worship services mirror the vast variety of nations present in our community. We grew to look and feel more like a well-represented community if you looked up front on any given Sunday, but I know something will be lacking on that front until that diversity extends to the preaching and administrative team working there all week.

Navigate Differences with Integrity and Grace

This requires that a church or an organization be very clear about who they are from the start. Immanuel church supported the ordination of women into pastoral ministry. We also practiced both infant and adult baptism. And while we affirmed that the charismatic gifts were valid, we also had a made a conscious choice to limit their expression in the context of a Sunday worship experience. We knew all of this represented who we were as part of our core identity as a church so when people came with differences of opinion on these matters, we were able to have clear conversations with them. On the matters of women in pastoral leadership and baptism, if someone came with a differing theological viewpoint on these issues, we were able to clearly state where we stood on these matters and why, and told them that while they didn't have to change their views, if they wanted to be a part of the community of Immanuel International, then they needed to be able to do so without being divisive or raising concerns about these matters. If they could do that, they were welcome. If they could not do that, then perhaps another church might be better for them. This is a hard thing to say to someone, but it's far better to acknowledge when a community may not be the best fit for someone than to fight a constant uphill battle of trying to get a person to accept who you are as a church. Welcoming newcomers doesn't mean that you have to shift your core identity every time someone new walks in the door, but it does mean that you need to have a clear understanding of which stances are core to your identity and which may be negotiable for the greater good.

For instance, it may be a high value to feature an organ in worship, but in order to welcome a newer segment of your population, you come to realize that perhaps adding a guitar and drums would be desirable for some. As a church, you will need to assess how feasible it will be to incorporate that change into your community life together and if it will indeed help you reach the central vision you have for your church. In the case of the use of charismatic gifts, when we met with people to discuss our life together as a church, we explained that while we affirm the validity of the charismatic gifts, we also felt that it hurt our community more than enhanced it to pursue the free and full expression of those gifts in our worship services. That is certainly a debatable point of view, but at the time we discerned that this was how our community would live best together.

Understand Differing Perspectives on Time

Understanding the differences in perspective on time is another key element in bringing diverse people together. The way different cultures interact with time is one of the more fascinating aspects of our diverse world. In many places of our world, time is a mere suggestion that has little to do with when something will start or finish. Time can create a major conflict when it comes to navigating differences. A prime example of this happened in our first year of ministry. We had formed a worship committee comprised of a very diverse group of people, including representatives from North America, Nigeria, South Africa, England, and the Netherlands. At one of the first meetings, the North American raised the issue of the length of our worship service. Her concern was that we were going too long, creating a problem for the Sunday School teachers (Sunday School being held concurrently with the worship service) and putting too much pressure on people to be at church too long. A few minutes later, the Nigerian arrived and stated, "I think we need to talk about the length of our service. It is entirely too short." Doug and I looked at one another and knew that this was a living metaphor for navigating differences in a meaningful way. We were able to discuss the issue with the entire group and concluded together that we needed to adhere to a service time that was within 75 minutes for the sake of our Sunday School and the overall enjoyment of the community.

For those from backgrounds who wanted longer worship services, we encouraged the continued development of our African Fellowship group who met on Saturday nights. Anyone was welcome, but it was called the African fellowship because they worshipped more in a West-African style. Doug and I did not impose any constraints on the length or style of that worship time. Over time, we also sought to integrate more music from different cultures into our Sunday worship service in order to celebrate a variety of styles. This allowed us to diversify our worship service while still operating within the parameters of an orderly framework that we felt served the community best.

The goal of an integrated community is to broadly reflect your population while discerning, building, and maintaining your core identity as a church. Differences are not to be feared but rather to be embraced because as we embrace one another, perhaps what we find is that amid our differences we are more similar than we ever thought possible.

Appropriate Assimilation

While we never want to require conformity for conformity's sake, there are times when asking those from a different culture or background to assimilate is essential. Whenever foreigners come to a new place, there are certain cultural standards and societal rules that must be understood in order for them to get along in society. Here are a few things we all need to learn when we want to make a new place of residence home.

Learn the language

No one disputes the joy that comes with learning the language of the place where you reside. In my case, I learned Spanish when living in Colombia and Swedish when living in Sweden. I even found I learned quite a bit of English while living in England! I picked up only a little vocabulary in France, but it was enough to get around, greet people, and order food in a restaurant. We knew our time there was limited, whereas I lived in Colombia for two years. Little English was spoken so I knew that if I desired a life outside of the small English-speaking community, I needed to learn Spanish. But here's the thing—it took time for me to learn the language. In the meantime, I needed patience and help from my Colombian friends. It was the same in Sweden. Over time I learned more and more Swedish but during the time when I was new to the language, I needed patience and help from my Swedish colleagues and friends. And I continued to speak English with other English speakers, which represented the majority of people with whom I interacted.

I was lucky. In both cases, I had friends and colleagues who were invested in my successful learning of the language and they helped me a lot. They sat and translated meetings. They didn't switch to English when I was struggling to speak their language even though I did so poorly. They offered to have conversations so I could practice. I mention this to illustrate the reality that learning a language takes time and energy and patience from not only those trying to learn, but also from the community around them. Too often we get angry with people for not speaking the language and offer no accommodation at all for the fact that they might be trying to learn but are struggling. This is discouraging and unwelcoming behavior. Yes, newcomers should be encouraged to learn the local language, but the key word is encouraged. Support them in doing so, and offer patience, translation, and help while they are in the process.

Understand that living in a culture with a new set of societal rules is exhausting

Offer people small respites away from these pressures and from feeling like a stranger all the time. This includes offering them, from time to time, the opportunity to be with others from their culture and language group without being offended that this means separating themselves from the whole. It just means they want to relax a little. Give them that space and it will encourage them to enter the foreign space with renewed energy. Remember, even your church, as welcoming as it may be, is still a brand-new environment for the newcomer. Anything you can do to ease their sense of feeling like an outsider will be a welcome gift and will encourage people to hang in there and continue to get to know the community better and better. Eventually, they will find their niche and feel empowered to step out of their own comfort zones to brave more uncomfortable territory.

Examine which social rules must be observed in order for a community to function well

As mentioned above, one of the most extreme cultural differences is our relationship to time. Some cultures manage their time to the second. Being late is a sign of disrespect and irresponsibility. But for other cultures, time is only a nod to the approximate time something will take place and showing up whenever is perfectly acceptable, even desirable in some instances. When these mentalities collide, it can be a recipe for misunderstanding, insult, and general relational disaster. For the sake of their common goals, a community must establish a culture of their own around how things will run.

More often than not, the cultural norms of the church's geographical position will prevail. In Sweden, things just didn't work if they didn't start on time. Being on time mattered, and strict adherence to when things started and ended was often necessary as we shared many rooms in the building. We had to emphasize to all who entered that we operated on Swedish time and if they showed up late, they were sure to miss out on something. In the cases of wedding and funerals, we repeatedly emphasized how important it was to start on time or else the church or the musicians were not going to be available. Sometimes this was quite difficult. But it was a necessary aspect of successfully managing our life and ministry together. We stayed committed to starting our worship services and other events on time so that people would eventually learn that this is how we did things.

The flip side of this is when someone from another culture hosted an event like a birthday party or a graduation party outside of the church, they were certainly free to run their event however they saw fit. When a family from Eritrea planned a graduation party for one of their kids, there would be a start time on the invitation, but we learned early on that, if we actually showed up at the designated time, we would be alone, sometimes for an hour or more. Everyone else was operating on Eritrean time, which meant—well, I still don't know what it meant! Being from a country where start times were firm, I never could fully grasp how people functioned with such an unclear system of when things started. But in this instance, it was their party and it was my job to adjust. In this sense, there was give and take. Church events and events in our home, operated on Swedish time. Outside events operated on the time that was appropriate to the culture hosting the event.

Adhere to the laws of the land

This may seem obvious, but it isn't always self-evident to a person who has newly arrived that the laws of the land that may differ from those of their homeland. When it's a matter of law, cultural nuances do not matter. When you are in a country with laws that differ from the laws of your home country, you must learn these laws and obey them or face the consequences. One law that foreigners in Sweden needed to be made aware of was the spanking law. Spanking in any form is absolutely against the law in Sweden and therefore, no matter your own personal opinion on the topic, it is not allowed. Parents needed to be informed that whether in public, or at church, or in their home, they were not allowed to touch their children as a means of punishment. We enforced this at church and spoke very seriously about this with our new families. There was simply no room for cultural interpretation in this matter. It is good practice to understand what laws may be unique to your local environment and implement ways to ensure that all newcomers are well informed.

Walking the fine line between assimilation and integration is challenging. There are, of course, areas in which people must assimilate in order to function better in their new place of residence. But it's also true that all newcomers need to be able to retain parts of what they have brought with them to their new situation. A community that only seeks to assimilate the foreigner can come across as wanting to swallow up the newcomers and erase all evidence of the cultural and personal identity they bring to their new homeland. We need to discern and help one another discern when it's best to adapt and when to remain true to our own traditions and beliefs.

If I'm honest, I can admit that there were times when we too stubbornly resisted the pressure to conform to the dominant Swedish culture, thus creating more conflict with our Swedish colleagues than was necessary. But I can also honestly say that part of what drove our resistance was their over-insistence that we do things the Swedish way. Compromise from both parties was necessary. Today, there is much more give and take at Immanuel church due in part to the resistance we employed that forced the Swedish leadership to re-think the manner in which they thought about and pursued integration.

As noted in chapter six, while tremendous gains are made when true integration takes place, when there is give and take from all parties, the costs can also be great. Everyone must be willing to change and therefore everyone must be willing to live with a certain amount of discomfort in the ways in which things will be done. For the dominant party, who is most used to having things their way most of the time, this will create the most discomfort. And it will require great discipline from the dominant party because it will require them to consciously give up some of the power and privilege that comes with being the dominant party and submit to the newcomer or minority point of view. But if everyone can learn to live with the discomfort that these kinds of changes will bring, the outcome will be richer than anyone could ever imagine.

PRACTICE MEANINGFUL INTEGRATION

Experiencing other cultures and perspectives, enjoying relationships with people from exceedingly different backgrounds, engaging in conversations where the points of view are vastly diverse only serves to enhance our lives, not diminish them. As we identify with the foreigner and stranger and understand their points of view, we are more prone to appreciate why they must fight at times to maintain their own cultural identity. A well-integrated community recognizes the needs and values of each party and seeks to incorporate practices that include both.

As you strive to walk this fine line, don't forget to celebrate the joy of being a growing community of unique individuals. In the midst of the challenges of intentionally welcoming outsiders while becoming more multi-cultural, it is essential to lift up the joys of doing this hard work. The next chapter outlines some specific ways to celebrate.

10

Celebrate Together!

ALL THESE CHALLENGES AND tight-rope acts can be daunting, can't they? Changes and sacrifices must be made in order to fully welcome outsiders and work intentionally at being an integrated, more diverse community. But there is so much joy too! That's why it's all worth it. This chapter contains ideas to help you move toward warmly embracing and fully welcoming people from all backgrounds to share their traditions by providing opportunities to celebrate the variety of cultures represented in your community.

Host a Fashion Show

Yes, the single most amazingly successful event we ever held at Immanuel was a fashion show! We found it honored the beauty and creativity of other cultures in a visually stunning display of fabrics, color, and style. We in the United States lack a traditional mode of dress, so a fashion show provides other countries and cultures the chance to display their cultural dress in a beautiful and unique manner. For fun, we did have Americans wear baseball uniforms and cowboy gear, but those outfits didn't hold a candle to the beauty displayed by the various African and Asian outfits. An additional bonus is that it also reveals the deep diversity of each country on their vast continents when so often all Africans and all Asians get lumped together as if they each were from a single mono-cultural region. If you do decide to do a fashion show, here are some guidelines that will ensure a successful event.

1. *Have people sign up ahead of time.* People should sign up ahead of time and submit a small description of the clothes they will be wearing and who will be wearing the outfit. This assists in creating the narration that will be used during the show. Couples and parent/child combinations should be encouraged but it is also great for singles to enter. In fact, it's a wonderful way to involve singles in an event since they often feel left out of church activities.

2. *Build a stage.* No matter how limited your space may be, you can figure out a way to create a catwalk where people can show off their finery. Ideally, you'll want to elevate the space for better viewing and have an area where a few turns can be done.

3. *Hold a rehearsal and require all participants to attend.* Synchronizing a fashion show with all its bells and whistles takes effort. Having a rehearsal really helps to get things coordinated. Run through where people will stay until it's their turn. Walk them through the runway and the turns so that participants become familiar with the space and feel more confident the night of the show. Have them bring their clothes to the rehearsal and leave them at the place where the show will take place, if at all possible. This creates less chaos on the day of the event. Plus, the rehearsal is a super fun time for the group to bond.

4. *Have a central coordinator and a narrator for the event.* The central coordinator will help people get in line and direct the actions the day of the show. The narrator will be the person telling the audience about the clothes and the country being represented.

5. *Choose music that represents the global communities that are on display.* This adds one more layer of depth to recognizing and celebrating the diversity that surrounds us in our communities. Many people are rarely exposed to music from other cultures and this is a great way to introduce new sounds to people.

6. *Have a blast!* Enjoy the show, the display of color and culture, the joy of people representing their homelands, and the fun of watching people shine.

I am not kidding when I say that this event was a huge hit, so much so that it became an annual tradition. At Immanuel, it was also an easy and fun way for us to integrate with the Swedish and Korean groups because they also have varieties of national dress. The joy that participants experienced was amazing. To see their big smiles, so proud of the clothing from their homeland, was such a treat. It was always awesome to see the diversity of the clothing from around the world. A fashion show gives people an opportunity to really show off something that they are very proud of in relationship to their homelands. For foreigners living in a strange land, this positive, excited feeling is not something that happens very often in their lives. So much of their energy is spent trying to fit in and learning the norms of the culture in which they now live, work, and go to school. This often means dressing in a more western style and dampening their own indigenous cultural expressions. With a fashion show, you really see the personalities not only of the individual participants but also of the countries and cultures represented. It truly was one of our best events and really helped to draw people closer to one another.

You've Got Talent!

Another amazing way to spend an evening together? A variety show. Every culture has its own forms of dance, music, art, and humor embedded in it. Why not invite people to come out and share their gifts at an evening of fun and fellowship? Much like the fashion show, it does require a bit of preparation, but the end result will be a dazzling display of often hidden talents. Many of the principles from the fashion show apply.

1. *Have people sign up ahead of time.* The sign-up form should include information about the act they'd like to perform, how long they think the act will be, and what will be required in terms of musical instruments, accompaniment, and sound.

2. *Have a coordinator who will act as the master of ceremonies for the night and keep the show moving along.* This should be someone who is at ease in front of people, and who can manage the crowd with some spontaneity. It keeps the evening moving along and provides a needed introduction to the various acts.

3. *Have some filler acts just for fun.* Silly magic tricks, group participation minute-to-win-it types of games, humorous little skits and the like, all help to make the evening more enjoyable. Humor is a great way to break down the walls between people and it's great fun to get folks to be a bit silly at times. So much of life is serious. This provides an opportunity to see people from a different point of view. The joy that emerges when people are able to show off their unique dance moves, make people laugh, or play music from their culture makes for a delightful evening.

Food!

Food is one of the most obvious ways that we celebrate diversity. Cooking classes and potluck suppers offer people the opportunity to experience another culture in wonderful ways. Potlucks were a real treat at Immanuel International with restaurant-quality ethnic food delighting our palettes. Again, this is a place where people take real pride in their heritage. Sometimes we set up the room so that foods from various parts of the world were grouped together but at other times we simply had long buffet tables where the beauty of the different foods was on full display for all to enjoy. Here are some helpful hints for a successful multi-ethnic potluck.

1. *Ask people to bring a national dish that serves about eight people.* The concept of a potluck is new to many people outside of the US and a short explanation helped them to understand what it is they were to bring. Asking people to bring a dish for about eight people worked out quite well with many bringing more than that and a few bringing less.

2. *Have people fill out a card identifying the dish.* The card should include the name of the dish, what country the dish is from, what the dish contains, and whether or not it is spicy. This will help people learn more about foods from the various countries of our world while ensuring that a food allergy won't be triggered inadvertently.

3. *Encourage portion control.* As you get started, offer a gentle reminder that people on the front end of the line should be mindful that there are many people coming through the line after them.

4. *Provide table settings and beverages.* It simplifies the evening if you can provide a few things instead of requiring everyone to bring all that is needed for the evening. If budget is an issue, charge a small fee or suggest a donation in addition to asking people to bring food in order to cover things like cutlery, beverages, plates, napkins, and decorations.

5. *Give thanks in a variety of languages.* No translation necessary. This serves as a good reminder of the vast global community that has gathered around the table fellowship that evening. Alternatively, put the same prayer on the tables printed out in a variety of languages.

6. *Tuck in and enjoy every morsel!* This is another opportunity to deepen our appreciation for other cultures and traditions. The stomach finds its way to the heart.

In addition to having potluck suppers, cooking classes are a fantastic way to introduce people to each other's customs and cultures. If people liked a certain dish at a potluck, it's a great follow-up to ask the chef of that dish to host a cooking class so others can learn how to make it. If you have a decent church kitchen, set up a weekly gathering for people to spend a few weeks either learning about one cuisine or switching the cuisine each week. If you lack a church kitchen, perhaps smaller classes could take place in people's homes.

Food is another deep expression of one's heritage and wonderful stories get told around a shared meal. Learning to cook together enhances fellowship and breaks down barriers between people. The ones doing the teaching get to bring their expertise to the group and the ones doing the learning get to be exposed to a new way of preparing food while getting to know the host in a manner that other situations may not have not allowed. The early church knew the value of gathering for meals and conversation. "They devoted themselves to the apostles' teaching and to fellowship, to the breaking of bread and to prayer" (Acts 2:42). Amen to that. Almost any activity that fits into the categories of teaching, fellowship, breaking of bread, and prayer serves to enhance the deepening of relationships and create a more integrated community. Keep an eye out for activities that are equally inviting for people of all cultures and invest there. The ideas are endless. You have only to use your imagination.

11

Embrace the Wider World of Christianity

MONOCULTURAL COMMUNITIES GATHER FOR worship to sing with tremendous gusto about our longing to join voices with people from every nation. Unfortunately, it is much easier to sing about every nation and tongue worshipping together than it is to actually pull it off. Many churches in the US remain remarkably segregated even though they often hear and declare the value of these words from Revelation 7:9.

> After this I saw a vast crowd, too great to count, from every nation and tribe and people and language, standing in front of the throne and before the Lamb. They were clothed in white robes and held palm branches in their hands.

Most Christians proclaim that the love of God in Christ is to include the entire world and that as the children of God we should be united. And yet so often, we fail so miserably to achieve this unity. What does seem to be true is that when people experience unity amidst diversity, that becomes normative for them and the desire for such strengthens. The majority of people I interviewed from international congregations mentioned that one of the more beautiful aspects of being part of such a church is catching a glimpse of what heaven will actually look like. Churches with broad diversity are hard to find in many places and most say that after experiencing life in an international church, going back to a homogenous church is quite challenging. Having tasted and savored the rich diversity of a multi-cultural community, a homogenous church now strikes them as bland and lacking in dimension. Experiencing the richness of being part of a community where differences are celebrated and enjoyed rather than feared drives a deep desire for people to seek out diversity when looking for other communities to join. This can have a cumulative effect throughout society.

Seeing the struggle that churches have had to diversify, I have often wondered why international churches in Europe have flourished. On paper, it looks like an experiment that would surely fail. The people involved come from over fifty different countries, with religious backgrounds that include Catholics, Orthodox and every branch of the Protestant church, in economic circumstances ranging from CEOs of top multi-national companies to refugees without documentation. How in the world could a church function with so much diversity and not be filled with conflicts and misunderstandings? The experience of being an outsider becomes a great common denominator. The fact that most everyone in these churches is a foreigner is helpful in instilling in people a deep desire to find unity amidst the diversity. All hunger for connection. Most long to find places in their new society where the language barrier isn't constantly in their face. An eagerness to find a place of worship where their faith can be nurtured in the midst of so many other life changes is ever-present. The deep desire to find a place to belong opens a willing spirit to embrace differences.

While these factors help to draw people into the church, keeping them around isn't always a done deal. Any church that is seeking to welcome a foreign or culturally diverse population should realize that an ethos must be created around welcoming not only new people but also new perspectives and ideologies. Connecting with others who are different will be difficult if one isn't open to experiencing new ideas. Everyone who comes into a diverse community must do so with a modicum of flexibility that allows space to breathe with one another when encountering challenging differences. A congregant from Immanuel remarks,

> Being part of an international church was challenging at first because the members not only come from different denominations but also from different backgrounds. I suddenly discovered that I was not as inclusive as I thought that I was. I discovered that I was very "privileged" in many ways and had prejudices too. Being part of the international church helped me truly understand what it will be like in heaven where Christians of the world will unite and praise God in different ways and languages. Being part of an international church has shown me that there is no one fixed recipe for what it means to be a true Christian; that getting hung up on water baptism as an adult or being baptized as a child does not make one a real Christian; that not speaking in tongues does not mean that one does not have the fruit of the Holy Spirit.[1]

If experiencing a taste of heaven means that a rich and varied diversity exists in the relationships formed within a community, then it follows that the longing for a taste of heaven is driven by an openness and curiosity about people who are different. The more open people are to experiencing the beautiful diversity that exists in our world, the greater the taste of heaven becomes. People learn to embrace a new way of seeing the world when meeting people from other cultures and backgrounds for the first time, instead of being threatened by those who are different. True curiosity and openness to others is next to impossible when we never meet anyone different. Our places of employment, our social circles, and our churches often lack any real diversity and so the richness that emerges when you interact with people who differ from you is largely lacking in people's lives.

It's easy to feel uncomfortable or threatened by difference. When we feel uncomfortable we often dig our heels even deeper into our own points of view. Having opportunities to build relationships with those who are vastly different invites us to open

1. Personal conversation, May 12, 2019

ourselves up to the world that Jesus wants us to inhabit: a world that reflects the entirety of God's creation, not just the one with which we feel most comfortable.

A German man who lived in Stockholm reflects on his experiences in the international church:

> Homogeneous groups are blind to many things. Being part of an international, diverse community helped me see God's presence in the world in new ways. Getting outside of my own culture revealed how church and faith are broader than my own nation's assumptions about being a believer. I feel challenged to consider what I believe and why since not everyone who surrounds me thinks the same way that I do. My faith changes and expands through meeting believers from different places. Experiencing Jesus in the lives of church members from all over the world breaks down borders, and lets me feel that God is greater than any nation.[2]

The church has an opportunity to be that place where people from different cultures meet and learn to love one another, providing that taste of heaven because of the common bond we have in Jesus. Interacting with different cultures helps us to learn about how God is at work throughout the entire world, not just in the backyard we inhabit.

The testimony of a successful Indian businesswoman reveals how participating in a diverse community helps us learn about ourselves as well.

> Most of the churches I belonged to throughout my life were homogenous churches where I did my best to fit in. I had to adapt my behavior and tone down the way I dressed in order to be accepted. The years before I first stepped into an international church nearly broke me. I did not fit into what was expected of a good Christian wife since I dressed in smart clothes and not in shapeless grey or subdued colors, did not volunteer to teach Sunday school, pursued a profession that was not that of a teacher or nurse but one considered worldly, a

---

2. Personal conversation, May 8, 2019

businesswoman. I also did not have children—even though I could have. I was not allowed to use the gifts that I had in the church. I was told I would be a distraction if I sang in the choir since I dressed too attractively. I was not allowed to participate in women's retreats since my ideas were too feminist and feminism was from the devil.

Then God led me to an international church where the co-pastor was a woman who was not only an excellent preacher but a very strong woman whose husband did not feel threatened by her but encouraged her. This was a vibrant and colorful church—where people not only dressed colorfully but where women served in ministries other than Sunday School. The women in this church were housewives, mothers, single women, wives who didn't have children, successful businesswomen renowned in their fields, and most of them spoke their minds and were independent. Suddenly I was not a tolerated foreigner anymore but a welcome addition to this colorful church. For the first time, I felt I was a part of a family and my uniqueness was not just accepted but appreciated and encouraged. I was invited to use my gifts in the church, too, and no one considered me a distraction anymore. About a month after attending this church, I suddenly noticed that I was no longer "dressing down" to go to church or toning down my temperament or the volume of my laughter. It was in the international church that I finally found healing for so many emotional and spiritual wounds that I had suffered in the church and outside of it. It was here that the shackles were broken, and I started to become the unique woman of God that God wants me to be.

The beauty reflected in these testimonies reminds me that having the opportunity to join with Christians who are different than we are ushers us into situations where we can not only broaden our limited perspectives, but also be affirmed ourselves in ways that our homogeneous communities sometimes overlook.

Fixing our eyes on Jesus helps us to overcome our fears and insecurities when seeking to cross cultural barriers to embrace someone different from us. Making our core identity as beloved children of God our common anchor provides the stability necessary for entering into new relationships. This is how the international church thrives amid the great diversity present in the congregation. We find our center in Christ, who died for us all, and we rejoice in our common identity: being created in the image of God to reflect the fullness of God together. Against this backdrop, the barriers between us get smaller and the differences between us more fascinating than menacing. A congregant remarks that differences become interesting. "They make you special. It's affirming when people are interested in your point of view and desire to hear what I think."[3]

When we appreciate our differences, conversations turn from people accusing others of being wrong to people exclaiming, "Wow, you've helped me think about that from another perspective!" Studying the Bible with people who have had different life experiences brings insight that others would never consider. A study of Exodus might reveal the deep feelings of alienation and fear that the Israelites faced. Sharing that study with refugees brings the biblical narrative to one's front door. The valuable insight gained from encountering people who identify personally with the emotions embedded into a biblical story might increase your empathy for those sitting with you around the table. Take any Bible story, read it with a diverse group of people and each one will focus on something different from the story because our varied backgrounds will lead us to resonate with different aspects of the narrative. This broadens our understanding of Scripture. Even though we may not always agree with the points someone else raises, at the very least, we are compelled to consider why we've come to the conclusions we have about a certain text. A colleague once observed, "When people from different backgrounds gather, we are forced to explain ourselves, and our backgrounds, and our ways of being Christian. We don't have the luxury of assuming things about each other."[4] Our understanding of and appreciation

---

3. Personal conversation, May 8, 2019.
4. Personal correspondence, May 9, 2019

for the biblical narrative is expanded and enriched by reading the Bible or engaging in theological discussions with people from different backgrounds and cultures because our traditions lead us to recognize a variety of emphases within the text. This helps us to see that the Christian faith thrives in a variety of cultures and isn't constrained by the cultural biases of our own homeland.

It's hard to notice the cultural bias that we bring to our faith unless we are exposed to other points of view. Those who come from oppressive nations where freedom to practice their faith openly will interpret and notice nuances in Scripture that someone from a more open society might completely miss. Hearing their take helps us to grow not only in our understanding of faith and theology, but also in our empathy for those lacking freedom to worship. Many from our church in Stockholm, for whom life was a constant struggle, clung to the texts that looked forward the day when all would be made right, suffering would end, and oppression would cease. Those of us who live comfortable lives here on earth have a harder time appreciating the hopeful future that scripture promises, where all needs are met and true justice prevails. When we examine texts about the poor and oppressed with the poor and oppressed we feel their pain and read God's promises with a fresh urgency. Discussing war and pacifism with people who fled Uganda under Idi Amin's reign sheds an entirely new light on the topic. Seeking to discern a "Christian position" on any number of issues will be a much more meaningful process when we do so in the company of people who bring differing points of view and a variety of life experiences to the table. I believe that we get closer to the whole gospel when people from the whole world gather to grow and learn together. Understanding more clearly how our culture has influenced our thinking helps us to become more open to a richer view of Scripture.

We all have to fight against our instinctive beliefs that our version of Christianity is the only true version. As one of of the people I interviewed put it:

> Getting to know believers from around the world allows you to drop your stereotypes and understand that there

is only one God, one Jesus. It is not helpful if every nation or church thinks that they know better than others because no one sees the fullness of Christ on their own.[5]

We can always learn something new and discover a different point of view on a topic or scripture. A long-time member of Immanuel remarks,

> The essence of the gospel is both much simpler and more all-encompassing that I realized; I needed to be in an international Christian community to see this in practice. There are many good ways of doing things, and no one person has all the answers, not even an Englishman from All Souls Church in London—honesty compels me to admit this! I needed to be in a multicultural Christian community, where all were committed to building up the body of Christ, to see this in practice, and realize how narrow-minded I had become.[6]

Cultures differ in their expression of Christian faith and how they prioritize issues related to their faith journeys. For example, the word evangelical is defined in a variety of ways by people. Many Christians throughout the world understand evangelicalism to be rooted in sharing the good news of Jesus Christ rather than being connected to a political agenda. Concerns about social issues have varying degrees of priority among Christian communities scattered across our globe. A segment of US evangelicals tend to focus a great deal of attention on the issue of abortion while many faith communities in Sweden rarely discuss the topic. The volatile relationship between Israel and Palestine is a prime example of a topic that would garner remarkably differing views when people from diverse cultures and countries sit down to discuss the issues. Understanding what it means to be born again differs from person to person. Faith tradition, culture, country, and family are all factors that shape our Christian world view.

Given the diversity with which God imbued creation, I find it beautiful to witness the breadth of interpretations of our faith

5. Personal correspondence, May 8, 2019.
6. Personal correspondence, June 24, 2019.

that inhabit our world. The key to learning to abide with those whom we disagree is to move away from conversations that seek to determine what is right or wrong and move toward accepting differences. One of the most important aspects of welcoming people from a variety of cultures is that people who have been part of a community for a long time will learn that their way isn't the only way and that different isn't necessarily better or worse, only—well—different. One's sense of the global church is greatly deepened when encountering Christians from other parts of the world. Maturing as a Christian involves not being threatened by people who disagree with our point of view. Persuading the other to agree with us is not the goal. The goal is to understand more deeply that God created a big, diverse world and that Jesus entered the world in all its diversity to meet each person in their own context.

Our lives and faith are enriched as we listen to and learn from someone who brings entirely different insights about God and about Jesus based on a point of view that is shaped by a culture, a country, and a faith tradition that may be vastly different than our own. Encountering contrasting ideologies while understanding that we all belong to the same God is one of the remarkable outcomes of journeying with others who come from a different background that we do. The amazing truth is that, in the midst of all of these diverse points of view, the one thing that doesn't change is Jesus. The gospel message remains the same: Christ lived, died, and rose again to save us from our sin, and to give us abundant and eternal life. We affirm that what we have in common is the love of Jesus and a love for Jesus. As we cultivate that shared center, the differences become less threatening, and we learn to enjoy a broader view of God.

This is one of the gifts of growing in the context of a diverse population. We learn to agree to disagree. We continuously remind ourselves and each other of who we are in Christ. We seek to live into the calling to be the body of Christ in the world. One of the most beautiful things about the core message of Christianity and the deep wonder of the word of God is that it transcends culture and place and allows the people of God to join together around the essential truth of Christ's life, death, and resurrection. We know the depth of joy that comes with celebrating every nation and tongue once we've experienced it. It's the taste of heaven that we all long for while still on earth. This needs to be celebrated and not feared! But it takes courage and openness to move from a singular perspective to a global one. In order to do this well, we need to interact with people from different cultural heritage and traditions while also being given the opportunity to share our own.

At the start of this chapter I mentioned that the common experience of being foreigners contributes to the thriving of international church communities. When a community from the host nation is seeking to welcome people from another nation, the equation changes a bit. Those from the host nation aren't dealing with the emotions and experiences of being a foreigner and therefore may not be as hungry for connection as those entering the new country or culture. The willingness to change and grow comes a bit harder to established communities. This is why it's important to build empathy with the foreigner and to learn to see the needs, experiences, and alienation of people living outside of their homeland. As we learn to identify with those feelings of alienation, whether they come from a geographical move or from an experience, we are motivated to create a more inclusive space, in spite of the challenges it might present. When we identify with the longing that people have to find a place to belong, our longing to minister to that need should increase. Welcoming people from different backgrounds provides an opportunity to expand our view of the gospel and experience afresh the exciting ways that God is at work throughout the entire world. We move from having a faith that is informed strictly by our own nation and culture to a faith that is shaped by Christians throughout the world.

12

Share the Good News

AT THE END OF the day, no amount of programming or Bible study will ensure that you are a welcoming community. People can have head knowledge that they find difficult to apply. We may think we want to be a more open and welcoming community, but perhaps if we look hard at the situation, what we really want is for people of diverse backgrounds to come and join us just the way we are, rather than just the way they are. We don't really want the chaos that will come with opening our doors to foreigners, strangers, and immigrants. But there are many things that we don't want that Jesus says we need.

In my experience, the calling to be a welcoming church is central to the gospel of Jesus Christ. It is a calling that should neither be ignored nor pushed aside. The gospel of Jesus Christ is good news and it is good news for the entire world, not just for people we like, or those who are like us. It's good news for the poor and struggling immigrant, whether documented or undocumented, who is seeking a better future for her family in a foreign and hostile land. It's good news for the refugees who, through no fault of their own, cannot remain in their homeland. It's good news for the expatriate who's been moved across the world to do a job for a company that most likely doesn't care much about his well-being as long as the profit margin increases. It's good news for the student who decides to study abroad for a whole variety of reasons but finds the new country hard to adjust to, lonely, and isolating. It's good news for the professional who found a better or more interesting professional opportunity outside of her native homeland. It's good news for your new neighbors, even if they look and act differently than you do. The good news of the gospel of Jesus Christ is good news for the whole wide world and we as the church, wherever we are located, are called to be a part of the greatest welcoming committee this side of heaven so all who approach our doors are invited in to hear and experience the love of God in Christ!

I have tasted and seen what joy and goodness comes from being a struggling foreigner welcomed into a church that embraces newcomers week in, week out. I have colleagues scattered across this globe working in international churches who are also blessed to witness these vastly diverse communities coming together around Jesus, and embracing all that Jesus intended for them. They are learning from worshipping with folks who are as different from they are as the night is from the day but who eventually become the moon and the sun for them relationally. I have sat around the table with Indians, Pakistanis, Americans, Dutch, Germans, Mexicans, Swiss, Swedes, Ghanaians, Nigerians, British, Indonesians, Kenyans, Eritreans, South Africans, and a host of others from this vast globe. I have laughed and cried over the most delicious food the world could yield while sharing stories of joy and heartache. I have been inspired by people's deep faith and God's great faithfulness exhibited in spite of great oppression. I have gained insights into Scripture and been challenged in my own faith journey. My life has been enhanced, and my faith more deeply formed, by the relationships I have forged with those who were once strangers.

Sure, there are frustrations, disappointments, misunderstandings, and hardships when trying to integrate diverse cultures and work together toward a common goal. Sometimes your backgrounds are so vastly different that you wonder how you will ever decide on a course of action. But the enlightenment one receives from journeying with people from a variety of cultures and communities is utterly mind-blowing and such a deep blessing that one can't help but smile in the midst of the challenges. You work a process, you seek to grow, you exhibit humility, you ask for forgiveness, you try different approaches, you learn new perspectives, sometimes you fail, and eventually you thrive as a community, not in spite of your differences but because of your differences. You thank God every day for the divine creativity that resulted in a world as vastly diverse as the one we inhabit. You say "Hallelujah!" because in Christ, there really is no east or west, no north or south, just one big family of God that learns to love one another with a love that is unparalleled and a joy that supersedes anything else we've ever known.

My reflections are rooted in the experiences I've had while living abroad and in the joy of leading and participating in international churches. My narrative focuses on welcoming the foreigner. Maybe your current situation doesn't offer many encounters with foreigners. Even so, surely there are strangers in your midst who are in need of compassion and welcome. While your context may look completely different, and some of the principles and examples from this book may need to adjusted to better fit that context, my hope for all who desire to become a more welcoming community remains the same—build empathy for foreigners, embrace the stranger, experience the joy of new relationships. Yes, the calling is high, God's great gift is how rich our lives become when we embrace the stranger among us.

Relationships with people who are different than we are help us to see the full image of God. We become less myopic and more generous. We feel greater empathy, engage in more meaningful self-reflection, and grow deeper in our relationship with Christ. These are but a few of the rewards that await us as we open up our hearts to people who are different. I hope you will see for yourself how embracing the stranger yields deep and satisfying growth in your life.

Many churches and ministries are doing amazing work with refugees and immigrants. Look around your community for ministries that are already engaged in providing a warm and helpful welcome to those struggling to find their way. A single person, a single church actively saying yes to expanding their community through the welcoming of foreigners and strangers serves as a catalyst for mobilizing others to do the same. As more members of the Christian community say yes to embracing the wonderful, diverse, multi-cultural world that God created, walls that separate people will come down and the opportunity that the church has to impact our world for good increases.

I really cannot imagine my life without the experiences and relationships that I have formed in the international church. I find myself pining for it when I'm away. I have come to appreciate diversity as the norm rather than the exception, and I am thoroughly grateful to God for allowing me the opportunity to live that reality. I hope that you will experience the stimulating challenges and utter joy that follows when your community more deeply reflects the beautiful diversity of our world. The church is well-positioned to be a place of welcome, that soft place for people to land, that warm embrace that people on the move are so desperate to find. Welcoming the stranger provides an opportunity for the church to open wide its doors, meet the felt needs of hurting people, develop relationships with people who will enrich its community, and build up the body of Christ. For so many people on the move, every day is filled with bad news. We who love Jesus have really good news to share. Let's welcome those in need as we have been welcomed: with the warm, accepting embrace of Christ's love. I pray that your church will experience what international churches in Europe are experiencing on a regular basis: that no matter one's background, no matter one's situation in life, all are welcome because God is our gracious host.[1] Amen.

---

1. Carlson, *The Covenant Hymnal*, No. 867.

Small Group Guide

Chapter 1: Recognize God's Concern for the Stranger

Read Leviticus 19:33–34, Zechariah 7:10, Psalm 14, and Matthew 25:34–36

1. At first glance, what strikes you about these ancient texts?
2. Who would you identify as today's widows and orphans? Who are the people our society tends to take advantage of if left unchecked?
3. Do you still think it's important for us to care for the widows and orphans and not exploit the foreigners among us? Why or why not?
4. Why do you think God's word is so emphatic on this point, repeating it several times throughout the Old Testament?
5. Often, Christians do not spend much time reading and pondering the Old Testament, even though it contains important principles that are still worthy of our attention and study. How do we interpret the Old Testament for our lives today? How are we to distinguish between culturally conditioned statements and biblical principles that God wants us to apply to our lives, no matter the place or time?
6. What are some practical ways that we could be living out Matthew 25:34–36?

SMALL GROUP GUIDE

Chapter 2: Identify with the Stranger

Read Exodus 21:21–22, Deuteronomy 10:17–18, and 1 Samuel 7:1–12

1. In these verses, God makes clear that the Israelites are not to exploit foreigners, asking them to remember when they themselves were foreigners. Why is the command to remember so powerful?

2. Where in your own life do you feel or have you felt like an outsider?

3. What has helped ease those feelings?

4. Have you encountered the concept of an ebenezer? Recall a memory of God's faithfulness during a time when you were feeling on the outside. Where do you need to raise an ebenezer so that when things get rough again, you will be reminded of God's faithfulness in the past in order to sustain you through the present?

5. What insight do you gain from identifying your own place of feeling like the alien or foreigner?

6. Does remembering your own pain motivate you to to ease the pain of others going through similar experiences of alienation?

7. What do you believe is the church's responsibility toward the foreigner/stranger/outsider?

8. Do you believe that those who live on the margins of our society occupy a special place in God's heart?

9. What are some practical ways that you can ease the pain of another's isolation or sense of alienation?

SMALL GROUP GUIDE

Chapter 3: Understand with Compassion

Read Ruth 2 and Ephesians 2:11–20

1. How did you react to the different versions of the Ruth narrative presented in chapter 3 of this book?

2. If you believe that God wants us to be more like Boaz, what are some practical ways we live into that calling?

3. Were you surprised to learn that there are thirty-six references in scripture about caring for the stranger/foreigner/outside among you?

4. What do you think would be the hardest thing about thing about living undocumented? Why do you think people are willing to endure that kind of stress?

5. Do you think the church's mandate to care should apply regardless of a person's legal status? Why or why not?

6. Why is it significant that the Gentiles are no longer strangers and foreigners, but should be recognized as citizens, as holy, as family?

7. How does this relate to the church's calling to ingraft people from different backgrounds and traditions into our communities?

8. Discuss the significant differences between philoxenos (brotherly love for the stranger) and xenophobia (fear of the stranger). How can a church move from xenophobia to philoxenos?

SMALL GROUP GUIDE

Chapter 4: Realize Who Moves

Read Genesis 12:1–10

1. What do you think Abraham and Sarah felt when they heard the Lord's call to leave their homeland? What would make it hard to obey this call?

2. Have you or someone in your life ever made a significant geographical move? Describe some early experiences. What adjustments did such a move require?

3. When you think of people who are on the move in today's world, who do you think of? Why do you think people make such significant moves? Under what circumstances could you imagine leaving your homeland?

4. Which of these stories increased your understanding of why people move? How do these stories increase your compassion for people who are on the move given the difficulties certain people face?

5. Consider how God might be asking you to "leave your homeland and go to someplace new." Maybe it's not necessarily in a literal sense, but rather in a figurative sense. Where do you think God is at work leading you to a new place?

6. What might God be asking you to leave behind in order to do something new and great in your life? Maybe it's an attitude, a relationship, a job, or the ways you use your time. What would it mean for you to say yes to God's call?

7. What do you think it means to be blessed to be a blessing?

8. List the ways in which you believe God is using you to be a blessing in another person's life, particularly someone who is feeling like an outsider. If you honestly cannot think of anything right now, then consider how God would like to use you as a blessing to another and begin to ask God to bring that about in your life.

9. Who are the people in your community who need a compassionate response to their circumstances? How is your church positioned to minister to them? What do you think they most need and can the church provide it?

SMALL GROUP GUIDE

Chapter 5: Grasp the Opportunity

Read Jeremiah 29:10–14, and I John 3:1–3, 16–17

1. What do you think about the notion that some people need to move in order to provide a more hopeful future for their family?

2. How does knowing that God's plans for you include a future filled with hope contribute to your own sense of belonging? Why is it so important to have a sense of belonging in life?

3. What other factors help you to experience that you belong? What are some obstacles that prevent people from enjoying a sense a belonging?

4. Why is it important for us to be mindful of our identity as children of God? How can we help others, especially the strangers in our midst, to claim this identity?

5. What are some of the struggles that newcomers face when they relocate? How are these struggles intensified when someone is a foreigner?

6. Why is the church well-positioned to help people develop a sense of belonging? How does it relate to our calling to love in action?

7. Name some specific ways that your church has an opportunity to minister to outsiders in your community.

Chapter 6: Count the Costs

Read Matthew 16:24–28 and Acts 10: 34–36

1. How do we take up our crosses in our daily lives?
2. In what ways might it be costly for your church/community to become a more welcoming community?
3. What feelings of discomfort get stirred up in you when thinking about welcoming in people who are unlike the majority of your church?
4. What are some practical ways churches can help people cope with the discomfort that comes along with change?
5. Discuss this statement: "Everyone must be willing to give up something that is important to them in order to make room for something different that is important to someone else." Why does this principle help us to be a more welcoming church? Does knowing that God shows no favoritism encourage you to be more open to another way of doing things? How?
6. Why do you think a measure of chaos accompanies a multicultural community?
7. How can you learn to celebrate the chaos instead of trying to quell it?

SMALL GROUP GUIDE

Chapter 7: Welcome Visitors In

Read Galatians 6:1–10 and Psalm 139:13–18

1. What does it mean to share one another's burdens?
2. What measures might a church working at becoming more welcoming adopt in order not to tire of doing what is good?
3. How does intentionally welcoming all visitors help you to reap a harvest of blessing?
4. Do you think your church is a welcoming church? What makes you say this?
5. Why would someone want to visit your church? What practices do you have in place that intentionally follow up with visitors and help them connect?
6. How can a congregation support its pastor in connecting with newcomers?
7. What makes a place feel welcoming? Where are these things made manifest in your church? Where are they not?
8. Does respect for all come naturally to you, or is it something you need to cultivate? What does it mean that we are all fearfully and wonderfully made?
9. What steps do you need to take as a church in order to cultivate an attitude of respect and care for all persons?
10. What do you think about the suggestions for being more welcoming? Are you doing any of them? What would you add to the list in your context?

Chapter 8: Distinguish Between Integration and Assimilation

Read 1 Corinthians 12:4–31

1. How does recognizing the variety and value of the different spiritual gifts help us to celebrate the diverse gifts that a community might possess?

2. How would you describe the difference between assimilation and integration? How is that distinction significant when seeking to welcome strangers/foreigners/outsiders?

3. Where in your community could you imagine a power struggle developing between people?

4. Have you ever been part of a community that exemplified either the model of the melting pot or of the salad bowl? What were the advantages of that model and what subset of the community enjoyed them? What were the disadvantages? Who suffered most from them?

5. What are some things that prevent a dominant culture from being open to new ways of doing and being?

6. What is gained by all parties through true integration compared to pushing for assimilation of minority groups? Did you find any of the examples from Immanuel Church to be relevant to your situation? Under what circumstances might it be better to operate ministries tailored to specific groups rather than insist that one size fit all?

7. If you are honest, where in your own community are you wanting to facilitate integration, but perhaps expecting a result that looks more like assimilation?

8. Why is a commitment to honoring the various spiritual gifts helpful in avoiding destructive practices of assimilation?

SMALL GROUP GUIDE

Chapter 9: Practice Meaningful Integration

Read Colossians 3:12–17

1. How does being tender-hearted toward one another encourage openness to new and different ways of doing things?

2. Identify the practices for a harmonious community as outlined in verses 12–15. Discuss how your church might translate these practices into specific habits that are more inclusive of newcomers.

3. How can church leaders nurture the value of sacrificing the comfort of homogeneity for the sake of welcoming people with diverse backgrounds? Why is this important?

4. What excites you about learning from other cultures/people groups that are different from your own?

5. Beyond the improved optics, how might the church be better served by becoming deeply multi-cultural in function and practice?

6. Why might it feel risky to ask newcomers to join the leadership/planning process?

7. What steps can you take to lessen the sense of threat and lean into the opportunities to include a wider spectrum of people in planning and leadership?

8. Discuss this statement: "Differences are not to be feared but rather to be embraced because as we embrace one another, perhaps what we find is that in the midst of our differences we are more similar than we ever thought possible." Why do we fear our differences? What do we gain by embracing differences?

9. Where do you perceive obstacles to becoming a more integrated community? List some areas where you desire to be better integrated within your own community. What is preventing you from getting there?

10. In what areas might assimilation actually lead to greater integration?

SMALL GROUP GUIDE

Chapter 10: Celebrate Together!

*Read Ecclesiastes 3:9–13, Acts 2:42–47
and Galatians 3:26–29*

1. Do you feel thankful that God has created such a vast kaleidoscope of people, cultures, and traditions? Are you glad that our world is so diverse? Why or why not?

2. What priority do you think God places on wanting us to enjoy life?

3. Why do you think things like a fashion shows, variety shows, and potlucks help people to understand one another better?

4. Do you think that sharing fashions, talents, and food from one's homeland helps a newcomer feel more comfortable in their new setting? Would it help you in that position? If not, what would?

5. What are some ideas that you could execute in your own community in order to celebrate cultural diversity?

6. What are some practical ways you can put Acts 2:42 into action in your own community?

SMALL GROUP GUIDE

Chapter 11: Embrace the Wider World of Christianity

Read 1 Corinthians 10:4–10 and Revelation 7:9–12

1. Why is the longed for unity of the church that Christ desires so often difficult to achieve?

2. What steps do we need to take in order to achieve such unity?

3. How do you think your own culture informs your view of Christianity?

4. Why is our point of view challenged or deepened by reading Scripture with people from different backgrounds? How does this contribute to our growth?

5. Is it possible, in your mind, for two people to read the same passage of Scripture and get totally different things out of it, due to their background? If so, how could we use such an occasion to grow closer and learn from one another rather than letting it drive a wedge between us?

6. Why does it take courage to move from a singular perspective to a global perspective? Is it essential for us to interact with people from other cultures in order to expand our worldview?

7. Does building empathy with a foreigner's experience encourage you to create a more inclusive space for them? Why or why not?

SMALL GROUP GUIDE

Chapter 12: Share the Good News

Read Luke 4:14–19, Acts 20:24, and 1 Peter 2:9–12

1. What is the good news of the gospel?
2. What does it mean that we belong to a royal priesthood?
3. Do you feel compelled, like Peter and Paul, to share the good news of Christ? What are some ways you can share the good news in your own context?
4. Do you believe being a welcoming church is an aspect of the good news of the gospel of Jesus Christ? Why or why not? How are you feeling at this point about becoming a more welcoming church?
5. What obstacles prevent you from reaching out to strangers, foreigners, and immigrants?
6. What are some ways that communities can thrive, "not in spite of their differences, but because of their differences?"
7. Who would you identify as the foreigners or strangers in your current context? What are some practical ways that your church could begin to reach out to these people?
8. How can you envision your image of God changing as a result of building relationships with people who are different from yourself?
9. Do you know of any other churches or ministries in your area that are reaching out to foreigners and immigrants? In what ways might you partner with them and support the work already in progress? In what ways might your church expand its outreach to fill a gap in existing services?

For Further Study

Hauerwas, Stanley, and William H. Willimon. Resident Aliens: Life in the Christian Colony. Nashville: Abingdon, 2014.
Labberton, Mark. The Dangerous Act of Loving Your Neighbor: Seeing Others through the Eyes of Jesus. Downers Grove, IL: Intervarsity, 2010.
Lanier, Sarah A. Foreign to Familiar: A Guide to Understanding Hot-and Cold-Climate Cultures. Hagerstown, MD: McDougal Publishing, 2010.
Law, Eric H. F. The Wolf Shall Dwell with the Lamb: A Spirituality for Leadership in a Multicultural Community. United States: Chalice, 2005.
McNeil, Brenda Salter. A Credible Witness: Reflections on Power, Evangelism and Race. Downers Grove, IL: InterVarsity, 2008.
———. Roadmap to Reconciliation: Moving Communities into Unity, Wholeness and Justice. Downers Grove, IL: InterVarsity, 2015.
Opstal, Sandra Van. The Next Worship: Glorifying God in a Diverse World. Strawberry Hills, NSW: ReadHowYouWant, 2016.
Rah, Soong-Chan. The Next Evangelicalism: Freeing the Church from Western Cultural Captivity. Downers Grove, IL, InterVarsity, 2009.
Volf, Miroslav. Exclusion and Embrace: A Theological Exploration of Identity, Otherness, and Reconciliation. Nashville: Abingdon, 1996.

Helpful Websites:

http://wewelcomerefugees.com
www.WelcomingTheStranger.com/Coalition
http://cwsglobal.org/

Bibliography

Bonhoeffer, Dietrich. The Cost of Discipleship. London: SCM, 1959.
Brouwer, Douglas J. How to Become a Multicultural Church. Grand Rapids: William B. Eerdmans, 2017.
Carlson, Richard. The Covenant Hymnal: A Worship Book, No. 867. Chicago: Covenant, 1996.
Carroll, M. Daniel. Christians at the Border Immigration, the Church, and the Bible. Grand Rapids: Brazos, 2013.
———. For Our Good Always: Studies on the Message and Influence of Deuteronomy in Honor of Daniel I. Block. Edited by Jason Shane DeRouchie, Jason Gile, and Kenneth J. Turner. Winona Lake (Ind.), 441–61. Eisenbrauns, 2013.
De La Torre, Miguel. "The Problem with the Melting Pot." Ethics Daily. February 9, 2009. Accessed October 19, 2019. https://www.ethicsdaily.com/the-problem-with-the-melting-pot-cms-13647/.
Gane, Roy. The NIV Application Commentary–Leviticus, Numbers. Grand Rapids: Zondervan, 2004.
Goldingay, John. Exodus and Leviticus for Everyone. Louisville: Westminster John Knox, 2010.
Hershberger, Michele. A Christian View of Hospitality: Expecting Surprises. Scottdale, Pa.: Herald, 1999.
Jones, L. Gregory. "Eucharistic Hospitality: Welcoming the Stranger into the Household of God," The Reformed Journal, March 1989: 12-17.
Moucarry, Chawkat Georges. "Aliens, Strangers, and the Gospel." InterVarsity. March 20, 2002. Accessed October 15, 2018. https://ism.intervarsity.org/resource/aliens-strangers-and-gospel.
O'Brien, Matt. "The Important Difference Between Assimilation and Integration." ImmigrationReform.com. December 28, 2018. Accessed October 06, 2018. https://www.immigrationreform.com/2016/09/29/the-important-difference-between-assimilation-and-integration/.

BIBLIOGRAPHY

Pohl, Christine D. Making Room: Recovering Hospitality as a Christian Tradition. Grand Rapids: W.B. Eerdmans, 1999.

Steves, Rick. Travel as a Political Act. Berkeley, CA: Avalon Travel, Hachette Book Group, 2018.

Tidball, Derek. The Message of Leviticus: Free to Be Holy. Leicester: Inter-Varsity, 2005.

www.ingramcontent.com/pod-product-compliance
Lightning Source LLC
Chambersburg PA
CBHW050825160426
43192CB00010B/1905